The history of

Royal Air Force Bentley Priory

and

Stanmore Park

John F. Hamlin

RAF BENTLEY PRIORY AND STANMORE PARK

This work has been produced at the request of the Advisory Panel for Local History Publications and was issued under the imprint of the London Borough of Harrow.

The panel was set up in 1977 at the suggestion of the Harrow Development Council for Adult Education, in order to encourage the study of local history, by recommending suitable works for publication. The current membership of the panel is: *Chairman:* Owen Cock, *Members:* Councillors Christine Bednall and Ann Swaine; Roy Abbott, Nikki Copleston, David Gibbons, Iris Long, Baj Mathur, Bob Mills, Peter Scott and Helen Shorter. Alan Hamlin, to whom this book is dedicated, was a long-serving councillor and member of the panel, and also Mayor at the time of his death.

The History of Royal Air Force Bentley Priory and Stanmore Park
First published 1997 by the London Borough of Harrow,
Civic Centre, Station Road.
Wealdstone, Harrow. Middlesex

ISBN: 0 901034 43 6

Copyright: John F. Hamlin

All rights reserved. No part of this publication may be reproduced, stored in a retrieval system, or transmitted, in any form or by any means, electronic, mechanical, photocopying, recording or otherwise without the prior permission of the publishers.

Printed and bound for GMS Enterprises by
Woolnough Ltd, Express Works, Irthlingborough, Northants

The author and publisher are indebted to many people and organisations for providing photographs for this history, but in some cases it has not been possible to identify the original photographer and so credits are given in the appropriate places to the immediate supplier. If any pictures have not been correctly credited, the author and publisher apologise.

RAF BENTLEY PRIORY AND STANMORE PARK

This publication is dedicated to the memory of Councillor Alan Hamlin

Mayor of the London Borough of Harrow 1996 - 1997

As a member of the Advisory Panel for Local History Publications, he was instrumental in contacting his namesake, the author John Hamlin and in initiating the publication of this history.

Alan's National Service in the Royal Air Force (1952 - 1954) took him to RAF Yatesbury and RAF Colerne near Bath, where he was a Radar Mechanic. He stayed there until he was demobbed with the rank of Senior Aircraftsman.

Alan had a great interest in books, history and in particular military history. He was a founder member of the Roxeth Local History Society.

The family interest in the armed services is being continued by his daughter, Lorna, his Mayoress, who during her year of office was also a Captain in the Army.

RAF BENTLEY PRIORY AND STANMORE PARK

Acknowledgements

My sincere thanks are due to those people who have provided help or reminiscences about time spent at the Priory or at Stanmore Park, among them the following:

Headquarters Air Cadets, RAF College, Cranwell
  Sqn. Ldr. Diana E. M. McCall WRAF (Retd.)
  Mrs Elizabeth Duncan (neé Trouncer)
  Mr. N. A. Greig MBE, for information on the Royal Observer Corps
  Mr. Harold V. Gross
  Mr Phill May.
  Mr. R. J. R. Mills, Library Services Manager, London Borough of Harrow
  Mrs. Elizabeth Pearson
  Mrs. Eileen V. Purle (neé Morgan)
  Mrs. Anthea Shepherd (neé Hammick)
  Mr. Jack Sherburn
  Mr. Graham M. Simons, for help with a variety of matters
  Mr. Bob Thomson, Local History Librarian, London Borough of Harrow
  Gp. Capt. Hugh Verity RAF (Retd.)
  Flt. Lt. Jim Walker BSc RAF
  Mrs. Mavis Warrender
  Mr Chris Way.
  Mr. Charles Willett
  Mrs. Beryl R. Williams, editor of the WAAF Association News
  Sqn. Ldr. Gerri Wilson BSc. RAF, Station Commander, Bentley Priory
  Wg. Cdr. D. H. Wood RAF (Retd.)
  Mrs. Ida Woolard (neé Goodwin)

Further Reading

'Dowding and Headquarters Fighter Command', by Peter Flint (Airlife Publishing Ltd., 1996) ISBN 1 85310 534 1

'A Nation Alone': The Battle of Britain 1940, by Arthur Ward (Osprey Publishing Ltd., 1989) ISBN 0 85045 935 4

'The Battle of Britain', by Richard Townshend Bickers (Salamander Books Ltd., 1990) ISBN 0 13 083809 8

'The Squadrons of the Royal Air Force and Commonwealth', by James J. Halley (Air-Britain, 1988) ISBN 0 85130 164 9

'They Shall Have Music', by Beryl R. Williams (Brigwill, 1995) ISBN 0 9525729 0 7 [the story of WAAF Voluntary Bands from 1939]

'Attack Warning Red', by Derek Wood (Macdonald & Jane's Publishers Ltd., 1976) ISBN 0356 08411 6 [the history of the Royal Observer Corps]

'Pilot, Diplomat & Garage Rat', by the late Air Cdre. H. M. (Toby) Pearson CBE (Merlin Books Ltd., 1989) ISBN 0 86303 445 4 [autobiography]

RAF BENTLEY PRIORY AND STANMORE PARK

Contents

Chapter 1	Before the days of Light Blue....	9
Chapter 2	The Royal Air Force arrives	19
Chapter 3	The war years	37
Chapter 4	Fifty years of peace, 1945 — 1995	87
Chapter 5	RAF Bentley Priory today	107
Chapter 6	Stanmore Park: the war years	111
Chapter 7	RAF Stanmore in peacetime	127
Appendix 1	Units	135
Appendix 2	Air Officers Commanding	137
Appendix 3	Station Commanders	138
Appendix 4	Properties requisitioned by the RAF	139
Appendix 5	Abbreviations	141

RAF BENTLEY PRIORY AND STANMORE PARK

Foreword

by

Squadron Leader Gerri Wilson BSc RAF

I was delighted when in December 1995 I heard that I was to be posted to Royal Air Force Stanmore Park as the Officer Commanding Administration Squadron. The Station, little changed in appearance since it was first built in 1937, like Bentley Priory, had a unique place in the history of the Royal Air Force. Indeed, during the last World War it formed the Headquarters of Balloon Command; controlling the activities of nearly 1500 barrage balloons - defending London alone required 450! The Station, the friendliest that I have served on, more recently supported the Headquarters of No 11 Group at Bentley Priory. Sadly, the draw-down of the Service meant that this character-full unit with its original, antiquated wooden huts was no longer required. Maybe it was time to move on - during its last winter the old buildings struggled to protect the modern equipment they housed; at one stage, we had more buckets in the Station Headquarters than we had computers! It was during our preparations for the Closure Ceremony that I became more aware of the history of both Stanmore Park and Bentley Priory.

The disappointment of the closure was of course eased by the fact that we would be moving to the prestigious site of Bentley Priory, home to the Headquarters of the newly formed No 11/18 Group. For myself the appointment to be the first Station Commander of the Royal Air Force's newest Station was a particular honour. Not only would my wooden-hutted office be replaced by one in a grand and historic building, but I would also be the first female to command a Station in the new Group. My interest in this fascinating book was naturally heightened by its many references to the involvement of members of the WAAF during Bentley Priory's history. Compared to my predecessors, there have clearly been numerous changes to life as a serving officer. Today there are very few areas in which you will not find women doing the same jobs as their male colleagues in a single Service no longer differentiated in title by our sex. At Bentley Priory, however, there are now only 32 Servicewomen compared to the 1120 of our predecessors who served here in 1942.

RAF BENTLEY PRIORY AND STANMORE PARK

It is appropriate that this book is nearing publication this month: each September we remember, and pay tribute to, those airmen who were killed during the Battle of Britain. Putting the book down for a moment's contemplation, I am compelled to look out of my window at the one time Fighter Command Headquarters - accompanied with its permanent guardians, a Spitfire and a Hurricane. The building is now used as our Officers' Mess and within it I have been privileged to meet some of the people whose exploits are recorded in the following chapters. The contents of my In-Tray are nowhere near as interesting, but currently include the final plans for a major building programme. You will read, and see illustrated, the many changes that have been made to the infrastructure of Bentley Priory over the years and, although we no longer need to requisition local, now extremely desirable, properties for accommodation purposes, we do need to make further provision. The site of RAF Stanmore Park will be sold in 1999 and consequently, the Sergeants' and Junior Ranks' Messes will be relocated in purpose built facilities at RAF Bentley Priory. This work will be completed by December 1998. Much of the remaining work will be to refurbish original, but recently unused, buildings for our various needs.

I leave here in December 1997 on maternity leave - another change since Dowding's days - and on my return will be posted to another station. Undoubtedly this has been my most enjoyable tour in the Royal Air Force and this book has helped to make it even more interesting. I depart sadly but in the knowledge that RAF Bentley Priory will thrive well into the next century and continue to live up to its historic past making a vital contribution to our air defence.

G Wilson
Squadron Leader
Royal Air Force Bentley Priory
September 1997

RAF BENTLEY PRIORY AND STANMORE PARK

Introduction

Over the years, many books and magazine articles on the history of Royal Air Force airfields have been published, among them several written by this author. Few works have been produced, however, dealing with the large number of RAF Stations which seldom, if ever, saw flying machines, although the work carried out at these locations may well have been just as vital to the successful operation of the RAF. This book, commissioned by the London Borough of Harrow, is an attempt to place on record the events which took place at two such Stations — RAF Bentley Priory and RAF Stanmore Park, with a number of nearby sites which came under their control.

Opened in 1926 in what had been built as a country mansion, RAF Bentley Priory was expanded several-fold during the Second World War when it was the Headquarters of Fighter Command and the ultimate responsibility for the defence of Great Britain rested on the high-ranking officers working there and on the personnel who backed them up so devotedly. With many modifications and updates, the task of this unique RAF Station remained similar during the 'Cold War', and since the easing of tension other units have taken up residence and are working on defence-related tasks. At RAF Stanmore Park demolition of another mansion took place to create space for the Headquarters of Balloon Command, which controlled the thousands of barrage balloons flown as a deterrent to low-flying enemy aircraft, thus supporting Fighter Command in the overall strategy. After the war, when balloons became redundant, the site at Stanmore Park was used for more mundane purposes until its official closure in April 1997.

I would like to personally dedicate this book to the gentleman whose concept it was — Mr. Alan William Hamlin, Mayor of Harrow for the year 1996/97, who in May 1997 died peacefully in his sleep with just one day of his term of office to serve. Although we had the same surname, I have not been able to discover any relationship. I sincerely hope that he would have been pleased with the result of my efforts.

John F. Hamlin
17th September 1997

RAF BENTLEY PRIORY AND STANMORE PARK

Chapter One

Before the days of Light Blue...

Few sites used by the Royal Air Force, certainly none of those still active, can have had such a long and interesting pre-military history as those described here. Although it is only within the last seventy or so years that the RAF has been in residence, both Bentley Priory and Stanmore Park had been established estates for many generations before the Service took over, and this Chapter recounts the events which culminated in the purchase of the two properties for development into the military assets which are the subject of this book.

Bentley Priory

Stated by Professor J. E. B. Gower in his book *'Place Names of Middlesex'* to mean land cleared of coarse grass for cultivation, Bentley was an area which was populated and had become civilised before the Romans arrived in England. Many artefacts dating from the Anglo-Saxon period have been found locally, indicating a thriving community in the area.

Soon after the Norman invasion, William the Conqueror invested Bishop Lanfranc as Archbishop of Canterbury and restored to the Church the land around Harrow which had been possessed by King Edward, recording the new ownership in the Domesday Book in 1086.

A Priory was founded at Harrow, probably in 1170 by a lawyer named Ranulf de Glanville, as a home for Augustinian Friars. de Glanville later became Chief Justiciary of England but in 1190 went on a Crusade during which he was the first English nobleman to lose his life. This original Priory is believed to have stood on the side of the hill, facing south, below the site of the present building, near Priory House on Clamp Hill. The Harrow Manor Rolls of 1512 state that the Priory was built in honour of St. Mary Magdalene and that the Archbishop of Canterbury gave the Priory and all its land to the Prior of St. Gregory without (i.e. outside) the walls of Canterbury.

In 1543 the possessions of St. Gregory were granted to Sir Thomas Cranmer, who immediately exchanged Bentley Priory and its land, totalling 329 acres (133 ha.) for land at Wimbledon owned by King Henry VIII. Three years later, the king gave the land to Robert Needham and William Sachaverell, and they in turn to Elizabeth Colte in 1547. Religious activity at the Priory then came to an end, and during the next two centuries the land changed hands several times before being sold in 1766 to a military clothing supplier, James Duberly. It is believed that it was Duberly who had the original Priory buildings demolished before having a substantial house, the nucleus of the present Priory building, built on the crest of the hill, the highest point in Middlesex.

James Duberly seems to have tired of his house and its beautiful site quite quickly, as he sold it in about 1788 to John James Hamilton, the wealthy 9th Earl and 1st Marquess of Abercorn, who commissioned several significant alterations to both house and surrounding parkland. In keeping with his new social status as Marquess, he employed the eminent architect Sir John Soane to enlarge the house and to make it "...*more lavish and sumptuous*". Except for the clock tower, the external appearance of the house is much as it was on completion of these alterations. Internally, the refurbishment included a fine staircase of Portland stone and a portrait gallery.

RAF BENTLEY PRIORY AND STANMORE PARK

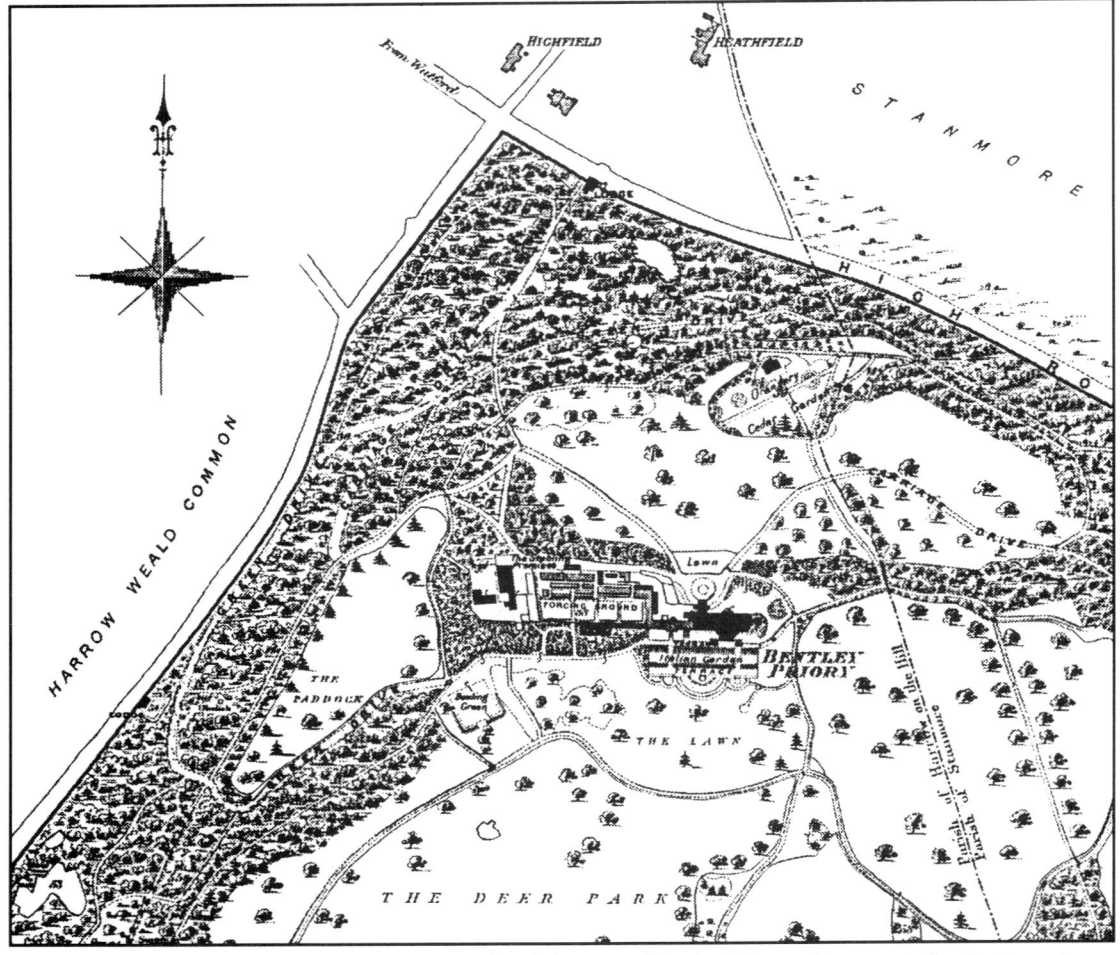

Detail from a mid-19th century map that gives some idea of the extent of Bentley Priory and its grounds. It only shows about half of the site - missing to the south is the lake, with its Boating House and Bathing House.

Further alterations followed in rapid succession, including the provision of a circular room or tribune lit from above in order to display works of art to their best advantage. Still not completely content with the extent of the work, the Marquess employed Sir Robert Smirke, who designed the British Museum, to carry out further extensions in the early years of the nineteenth century.

Bentley Priory soon became a favourite place for well-known politicians and artistic celebrities of the time to visit. The Marquess, a typical nobleman of his period, welcomed such luminaries as William Pitt, the Duke of Wellington, Lord Liverpool, the poet Wordsworth, Sir Walter Scott, Lady Emma Hamilton and actress Sarah Siddons through the portals of Bentley Priory. However, the Marquess suffered a very unhappy domestic life through his marriage to Catherine Copley, in whose family tuberculosis was endemic. She did, however, give him six children before she died in 1791. He then married his cousin Cecile Hamilton, but divorced her after she eloped six years later. His third marriage was to a widow, Lady Anne Hatton, in 1810. Apart from his legitimate children, there were two by his mistress, Frances Hawkins. In the Priory grounds a terra-cotta monument is dedicated to one

BEFORE THE DAYS OF LIGHT BLUE...

of the latter, John James Hamilton, who died at eight years of age. Ill fortune persisted, the Marquess losing every one of his children and three of his grandchildren over a period of eleven years. Unable to come to terms with these awful tragedies, the Marquess himself died, aged 62, in 1818, when the Earldom passed to a surviving grandson, seven-year-old James, whose guardian was Lord Aberdeen, his uncle by marriage, who married Lord Hamilton's widow in 1815, thus becoming the 2nd Marquess' stepfather!

The attractions of Bentley Priory became for the 2nd Marquess something of a liability due to the constant demands of visitors, many of whom tended to outstay their welcome. He therefore spent less time there than his father had, and before long his family became wanderers, until in 1874 they settled at Barons Court in Ulster.

Meanwhile, in 1846, the Dowager Queen Adelaide, widow of William IV, leased Bentley Priory, moving in two years later, by which time she was suffering from dropsy. Owing to her physical difficulties she lived on the ground floor until she died in 1849. The Priory then saw little use until in 1863 the estate was sold to Sir John Kelk, a railway engineer and contractor who built the Albert Memorial (free of charge!). Without delay he began to spend money on improvements to the building, and it was he who added the clock tower as well as a picture gallery, orangery, a portico and a library and in the grounds a deer park and a number of cedar trees.

Described as a 'palatial and unique mansion with about 466 acres' (189 ha.), Bentley Priory was offered for sale on 20 June 1880 by Driver & Co. but apparently failed to find a buyer. After living at Bentley Priory for less than twenty years, Sir John managed to sell the property in 1882 to Mr. Frederick Gordon, who converted the building into a hotel and in the grounds built a new house, *'Glenthorn'*, for his family's use. As access to the Priory from other parts left something to be desired, Gordon had a railway built from Harrow to Stanmore for the use of guests, at a cost of £48,000. Opened on 18 December 1890, the line was operated by the London & North Western Railway on behalf of Gordon's subsidiary company, the Harrow & Stanmore Railway Company. Some remains of the station can be seen as part of a newer building which stands at the junction of Old Church Lane and Gordon Avenue, Stanmore. An attempt to sell the hotel was made in June 1895 by estate agents Debenham, Tewson, Farmer

Early photographs can be hard to come by and are of very variable quality - some of the best images to survive were originally reproduced as postcards. Here Stanmore Village railway station, seen here in about 1910, was built to aid travellers to Bentley Priory, then a hotel.
[Harrow local history collection]

RAF BENTLEY PRIORY AND STANMORE PARK

Watched by a master, schoolgirls practice their putting on the lawn below the Italian garden at Bentley Priory, circa 1920. [Crown copyright]

& Bridgewater but failed when the property did not reach its reserve price, so the business, never a great financial success, carried on until the death of Mr. Gordon in 1908.

Bentley Priory then took on a new lease of life as a boarding school for seventy young ladies. They were well provided for, with twenty pianos in sound-proofed rooms being a feature! In front of the main entrance twelve lawn tennis courts were laid out. Any male staff working there were obliged to leave the premises by 9.30 p.m., when the gates were locked! The school survived the First World War, but failed in the financial slump which followed, and closed on 23 December 1924, after which the estate was unoccupied until being split into two lots for sale. On 25 March 1926 the Priory building and 40 acres (16.2 ha.) of land were purchased by the Air Ministry for about £25,000, while the remainder of the estate, amounting to 240 acres (97 ha.) was sold to a syndicate

Complete with potted palms and a Bluthner grand piano, the Drawing Room at Bentley Priory during its girls' school days seems to have been something of a hangover from Edwardian times. [RAF Bentley Priory]

12

BEFORE THE DAYS OF LIGHT BLUE...

Otherwise known as the Orangery or the Conservatory, the Winter Garden stood on the south side of the Priory building and was demolished during the early years of RAF occupation to make way for more practical buildings.
[RAF Bentley Priory]

BENTLEY PRIORY SCENES

This picture of the entrance hall to the Priory, taken in the early 1920s, shows the ornate furnishings of the period. Compare with a 1997 photograph of the same room in Chapter 5.
[RAF Bentley Priory]

Obviously posing for this picture are some of the girls who attended the Priory when it was a school. The gymnasium seems to have been fairly well equipped.
[RAF Bentley Priory]

RAF BENTLEY PRIORY AND STANMORE PARK

A classroom, perhaps the only one as it is referred to as the Lecture Hall, at Bentley Priory during its days as a girls' school. There are 48 desks, possibly enough to accommodate all the girls not engaged in other forms of tuition. A piano, a vital piece of equipment at the time, stands on the left side of the room.
[RAF Bentley Priory]

WHEN IT WAS A GIRLS SCHOOL

The Circular Room in the Priory as it was in the early 1920s. Today the room contains little furniture but portraits of aviation personalities grace the walls.
[RAF Bentley Priory]

The girls who boarded at the Priory seem to have lived well, if this picture of the Dining Room is indicative. [RAF Bentley Priory]

BEFORE THE DAYS OF LIGHT BLUE...

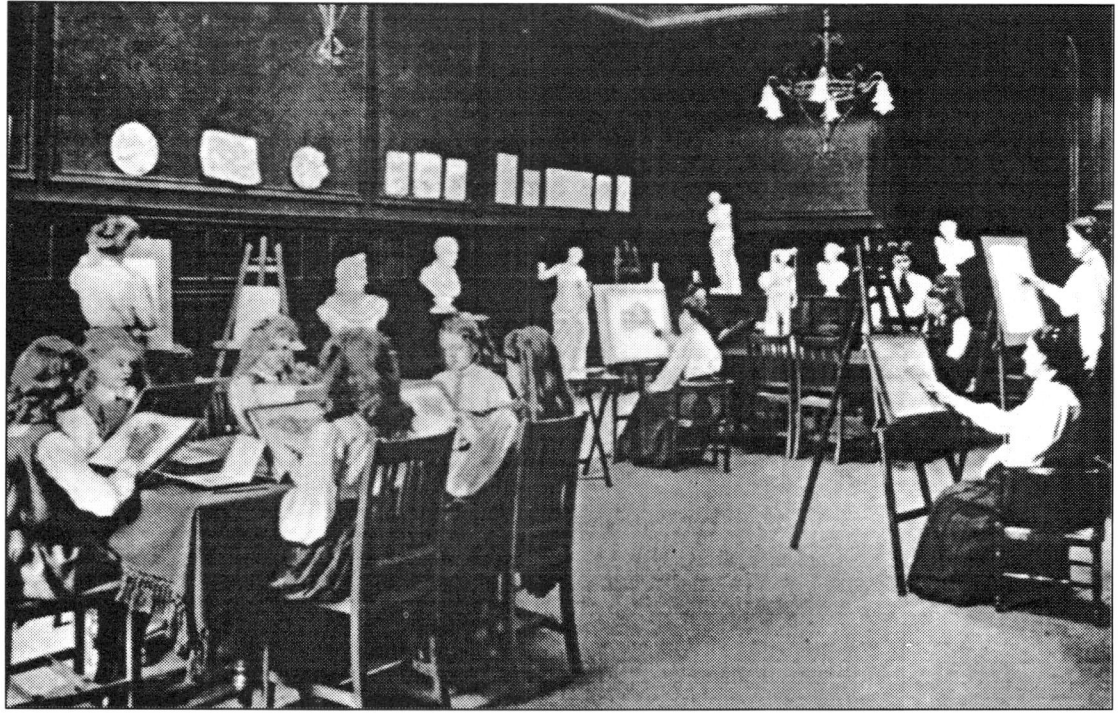

An art class under way in the school which occupied Bentley Priory from 1908 to 1924. [Crown copyright]

for division into building plots. Ninety acres (36.4 ha.) were purchased by Middlesex County Council, and this land remains an open space.

Thus it was that the historic Bentley Priory and part of its extensive estate came into the hands of the Royal Air Force, with whom it was destined to play an absolutely vital part in the defence of the United Kingdom during and after the Second World War.

Stanmore Park
The pre-history of RAF Stanmore Park is quite different from that of RAF Bentley Priory in that the original building, a large mansion, was completely demolished when the Air Ministry purchased the estate.

Stanmore Manor was presented to the Count of Mortain by William the Conqueror, his half-brother, soon after the Norman invasion in 1066. It is mentioned in the Domesday Book and is assumed to have been located near the present Old Church Lane. On the estate, by then owned by the Francis family, a manor house was built in the middle of the 13th century by Abbot John of St. Albans. In 1362 the manor was acquired, with 67 acres (27 ha.) of land, by St. Bartholomew's Priory, which already owned the adjacent manor at Little Stanmore. The dissolution of the monasteries in 1536 caused the Priory to become a secular property, and two years later it was leased by Thomas Wilkinson to Geoffrey Chamber for the sum of £13-13-4 (£13.67) rent per annum.

The manor at Stanmore consisted at this time of two tenements with gardens, orchards and pastures, two closes of arable land and twenty acres (8.1 ha.) of free land, plus fisheries. By 1542 Geoffrey Chamber seems to have acquired the freehold, as in that year he sold the property to King Henry VIII for £400. Chamber appears to have developed the property while it was in his possession, as by the time of the sale it consisted of a large area of agricultural land, as well as heathland, meadow, 1005 rents in Great

RAF BENTLEY PRIORY AND STANMORE PARK

Stanmore Park house from the north. [Harrow local history collection]

and Little Stanmore and a church. The King granted the manor to Sir Peter de Gamboa for services rendered, but when he was murdered in 1550 the property reverted to the Crown. It was leased by Queen Elizabeth I to a number of tenants and over the succeeding hundred years changed hands many times, until in 1713, in the reign of Queen Anne, it passed to the Earl of Caernarvon, who became the first Duke of Chandos. Great and Little Stanmore estates now united under a common Lord of the manor.

The land which became known as Stanmore Park was purchased in the 1720s by Andrew Drummond, fifth son of Sir John Drummond and a banker by profession. Several years later he commissioned John Vardy and William Chambers to design for him a fine mansion, Stanmore House, with grounds laid out by the famous 'Capability' Brown. When Andrew died in 1769 the estate was inherited by his son John, who suffered poor health and died only five years later. George Drummond, John's son, inherited the property but after spending a great deal of money unwisely on the estate died in 1788 leaving large debts.

Next to own the property was George

Stanmore Park house from the south during the period when it was a school. [Harrow local history collection]

BEFORE THE DAYS OF LIGHT BLUE...

Five-seat desks lined up in a classroom at Stanmore Park during its days as a school. [Harrow local history collection]

Harley Drummond, who attended Harrow School and inherited his grandmother's fortune, but he was wild and financially irresponsible. Eventually he was made bankrupt and having sold Stanmore House fled to Ireland.

The mansion was occupied in 1815 by Lady Aylesford and then by Lord Castlereagh, the Foreign Secretary and Leader of the House of Commons. After the Napoleonic Wars there was much hardship among ordinary people, caused by high taxation and poor harvests, and legislation was introduced to suppress public unrest. The unfortunate Lord Castlereagh, extremely unhappy at the situation, eventually took his own life.

In 1840 Stanmore Park was bought by the Marquis of Abercorn, but sold by him eight years later. By that time consisting of over 1400 acres (567 ha.) of land including a home farm, the property was purchased by Mr. George Carr Glyn, a partner in the banking concern Glyn, Mills, Currie & Co. For many years a director of the London & North Western Railway and MP for Kendal, he became the first Lord Wolverton in 1869. After his death in 1873 his son, George Grenfell Glyn, succeeded him, and eventually became Postmaster General. He offered the ten-bedroom property, described by

Boys at the cricket nets on the south side of Stanmore Park. [Harrow local history collection]

RAF BENTLEY PRIORY AND STANMORE PARK

A scene showing the demolition of Stanmore Park house in May 1938. [Harrow local history collection]

agents Daniel Smith, Son & Oakley as 'a large classic family mansion', for sale on 6 June 1884, complete with 57 acres (23 ha.) of land.

Stanmore Park then became a boys' preparatory school run by Mr. Kemball Cook, and remained so for fifty years until the school moved to Hertford in 1937, after which the house and estate was put up for sale. It was purchased by the Air Ministry who, in an action seen by many local residents as as act nothing short of vandalism, quickly demolished the house and destroyed the extensive gardens designed so long before by 'Capability' Brown. Although Stanmore Park estate was no more, its site entered an era of great importance in the history of the Royal Air Force.

RAF BENTLEY PRIORY AND STANMORE PARK

Chapter Two

The Royal Air Force Arrives

The purchase of the Bentley Priory property having been completed, the Royal Air Force was in a position to occupy the site at the end of May 1926, and so on 1 June the command element known as HQ Inland Area moved in from Hillingdon House, Uxbridge. Inland Area's AOC was AVM T. I. Webb-Bowen CB CMG, and the HQ controlled 21, 22 and 23 Groups, which between them looked after army co-operation and training units. On 1 November, however, AVM Webb-Bowen handed over command of Inland Area to AVM C. A. H. Longcroft CB CMG DSO AFC.

Due to the effects of the recent General Strike, alterations to provide living accommodation for officers and other ranks had not been completed in time and not all the essential services were operating fully. A shuttle bus service was therefore arranged to carry staff from and to Uxbridge every day. It was 22 November before the men could move into Bentley Priory dormitories. For the officers, a Mess was opened on 1 December in which

An aerial view of Bentley Priory taken in 1928, when the estate was still in its original condition. The conservatory which had to be demolished during the Second World War is prominent in this picture. To the north the area was, and to a certain extent still is, heavily wooded. [Harrow local history collection]

the occupants quickly settled down to their comfortable routine.

Chief Staff Officer at HQIA was Air Cdre. Drew, but he was succeeded on 12 December 1927 by Air Cdre. J. L. Forbes OBE. He in turn left on 22 January 1929 to take over command of the RAF in Malta, and two months later Air Cdre. A. M. Longmore CB DSO stepped into his shoes. This post seems to have been a somewhat transitory one, as Longmore left on 15 October 1929 to take command of the RAF College at Cranwell, and was succeeded by Air Cdre. W. R. Freeman DSO MC.

After nearly three and a half years in the post of AOC Inland Area, AVM Longcroft retired on 1 November 1929 and was replaced by AVM A. E. Borton CB CMG DSO AFC. A year later Gp. Capt. C. E. Rathbone DSO took over as Chief Staff Officer and was promoted to Air Cdre. on 1 January 1931. In April his title was altered to Senior Air Staff Officer, a term which has lasted to this day.

Towards the end of 1931 permission was requested by European Sound Films Ltd., a proponent of the new 'talkies', to build a film studio costing £175,000 on part of the Bentley Priory land. Hendon Rural District Council refused permission for this venture, and an appeal was lodged with the Ministry of Health, which dismissed it, arguing quite rightly that the area was predominantly residential.

Changes of organisation and command continued through the early part of the 1930s, the lull before the storm! Air Cdre. Rathbone left in January 1932 to become AOC RAF Mediterranean Area and was succeeded as SASO by Air Cdre. J. B. Bowen OBE, but he in turn left on 15 March 1933 to be replaced by Air Cdre. C. D. Breese CB AFC. Of greater significance was the return on 1 February 1933 as AOC Inland Area of Arthur M. Longmore CB DSO, who had been promoted to Air Vice Marshal since he had been Chief Staff Officer at Bentley Priory for a short time in 1929.

A new unit added to 21 Group on 2 August 1932 was the Aircraft Storage Unit, formed that day at Peterborough. The School of Stores Accounting and Storekeeping moved to Cranwell, and out of Inland Area jurisdiction, on 1 December 1932, and Coast Defence Cooperation

Headquarters Inland Area - early 1932

21 Group (HQ West Drayton)
Reception Depot, West Drayton *
RAF Depot, Uxbridge
School of Stores Accounting & Storekeeping, Kidbrooke
Record Office, Ruislip *
Aeroplane & Armament Experimental Establishment, Martlesham Heath. *
Home Aircraft Depot, Henlow. *
1 Stores Depot, Kidbrooke. *
2 Stores Depot, Altrincham. *
3 Stores Depot, Milton. *
4 Stores Depot, Ruislip. *
15 Squadron, Martlesham Heath. (part of A&AEE)
22 Squadron, Martlesham Heath. (part of A&AEE)

22 Group (HQ Farnborough)
School of Photography, Farnborough. *
School of Army Cooperation, Farnborough.
School of Balloon Training, Farnborough.
Coast Defence Cooperation Flight, Eastchurch.
2 Squadron, Manston.
4 Squadron, Farnborough.
13 Squadron, Netheravon.

16 Squadron, Old Sarum.
26 Squadron, Catterick.

23 Group (HQ Grantham)
Central Flying School, Wittering.
2 Flying Training School, Digby.
3 Flying Training School, Spittlegate.
5 Flying Training School, Sealand.
Packing Depot, Sealand.*
Station HQ, Manston.
School of Technical Training (Men), Manston.*

Air Armament School, (HQ Eastchurch)
1 Armament Training Camp, Catfoss.
2 Armament Training Camp, North Coates Fitties.
3 Armament Training Camp, Sutton Bridge.

Administered directly by HQIA
RAF Netheravon (for units of the Fleet Air Arm only)
Air Ministry W/T Section.*
Central Band of the RAF.*

NB - Units marked with asterisk (*) technically administered by Air Ministry.

THE ROYAL AIR FORCE ARRIVES

A flight of seven Gloster Gauntlets from 19 Squadron, RAF Duxford near Cambridge, with K4091 closest to the camera.

Flight was transferred to Coastal Area control on moving to Gosport on 23 May 1933. At Digby, 2 FTS began to close down in July 1933, leaving that Station on Care & Maintenance.

In November 1933 the Government admitted that its postwar policy of cutting expenditure on armaments had been an error of judgement which would now have to be corrected. Great Britain had only 850 military aircraft of all types compared with France, which had 1650 and Italy with 1000. No references to the aircraft which Germany was building surreptitiously or the pilots being trained covertly for the Luftwaffe were made, as the perceived threat was not from that quarter.

A new Group known as Armament Group was formed at Eastchurch on 1 February 1934 to take over from the Air Armament School control of 1, 2 and 3 Armament Training Camps and the Temporary ATC at Leuchars. The new Group was placed under HQIA administration but the training syllabus was controlled directly by the Air Ministry.

From 1 February 1934, when 21 Group HQ closed down, all its units came under the direct control of HQIA. Other alterations which took place in 1934 included the departure of 22 Squadron to Donibristle as part of Coastal Area and 15 Squadron to Abingdon to become part of Central Area.

AVM Longmore left on 30 September 1934 to become AOC of Coastal Area and was replaced temporarily by Air Cdre. Henry Le M. Brock CB DSO, the AOC of 22 Group. He in turn was succeeded by AVM Charles S. Burnett CB CBE DSO on 8 January 1935, just before the effects of the RAF Expansion Scheme began to be felt at Inland Area. On 1 April 1935, the 17th birthday of the RAF, HQ Inland Area at Bentley Priory was staffed by 30 officers, four Warrant Officers, 41 NCOs and other ranks, and 68 civilians, a small fraction of the numbers which would serve at the Priory in later years.

Expansion of the Royal Air Force

Following the announcement made in November 1933, a further statement was

RAF BENTLEY PRIORY AND STANMORE PARK

The Bristol Bulldog was used by a number of squadrons, this being an example from the famous 'Treble-One'.

made in July 1934 announcing massive expansion of the RAF. The aim was to have 41 new squadrons to give a total of 1310 aircraft by 1938. Still no threat from Germany was mentioned.

At Digby, the short period of Care & Maintenance on the Station ended on 1 October 1934, when 2 FTS re-formed in 23 Group. A further flying school, 6 FTS, came into being at Netheravon on 1 April 1935, and on 1 July the School of Technical Training at Manston became 3 SoTT as part of an expanding training system. To cope with an anticipated influx of recruits, a sub-depot of the RAF Depot was set up in August 1935 at Orpington in Kent. The Central Flying School moved in August from Wittering to Upavon, an airfield which was then transferred from Coastal Area to Inland Area control. At Wittering, after a short period of inactivity, 11 FTS was formed on 1 October 1935 and allocated to 23 Group.

More facts about expansion were announced in May 1935, when it was stated that the RAF was to be trebled in size in two years! No less than 920 new aircraft would be purchased. At the same time it was stated that since the expansion plans were first released no less than 29,000 men had applied to join the RAF.

To deal more efficiently with the rapidly increasing numbers of pupil pilots for whom Inland Area was responsible, a new syllabus was introduced at the end of 1935. Instead of spending five months on an elementary aircraft type and a further five months on an advanced type, pupils would henceforth fly an elementary type at a civilian-operated Elementary & Reserve Flying Training School for two to three months, then go to Uxbridge for two weeks' disciplinary training, followed by three months on a service aircraft type and finally three months advanced training at a Service Flying Training School.

Inland Area took over control of Hawkinge on 4 November 1935 when that Station became part of 22 Group, replacing Manston, which from 1 December came under the direct control of HQIA. Next day another flying school, 7 FTS, was formed at Peterborough, from where on 16 December the Aircraft Storage Unit (1 ASU) departed to Waddington and out of HQIA jurisdiction. A similar unit, 3 ASU, had been formed at Sealand on 2 December in 23 Group, administered by HQIA and the Air Ministry. On 16 December recently-reformed 48 Squadron moved from Bicester to Manston to act as the flying element of the School of Air Navigation, formation of which was imminent. On the same day, staff at North Coates formed a Station Headquarters to administer a new school for observers, 2 Armament Training Camp and the firing ranges at Donna Nook and Theddlethorpe.

THE ROYAL AIR FORCE ARRIVES

As part of a major reorganisation of the Observer Corps, which had been formed in 1925, two administrative areas, Southern and Northern, were set up in 1935, each controlling a number of Groups. Southern Area came into being at Bentley Priory, under the command of Gp. Capt. I. T. Courtney CBE, but in 1936 the Area organisation moved to RAF Uxbridge, where the Corps' headquarters was located.

The Expansion Scheme, gathering momentum, prompted the formation of several more Inland Area units during the early part of 1936. Two flying schools, 8 FTS at Montrose and 10 FTS at Ternhill, were formed on 1 January, as was the Air Observers School at North Coates, which was effectively the transfer of the Temporary Armament Training Camp from Leuchars. The School of Air Navigation came into being at Manston on 6 January by amalgamation of the Air Navigation School from Andover and the Navigation School from Calshot, but on 17 February 22 Group was removed from Inland Area and added to the organisation known as Air Defence of Great Britain (ADGB). Yet another FTS, 9 FTS, was formed at Thornaby on 2 March, when that Station was transferred from ADGB to Inland Area control.

By now, the rapid expansion of the Royal Air Force had caused a major administrative problem, as several different functions, some operational and others not, were being handled by each first-line body. It was therefore decided that henceforth the organisation of the RAF would be in Commands, each having a specific role to play rather than a general function. Thus it was that on 1 May 1936 Inland Area, by then in control of 23 Group and Armaments Group, was renamed Training Command, and 23 Group became 23 (Training) Group. However, Bentley Priory had a different part to play, and to allow it to happen HQ Training Command moved on 10 July 1936 to a new home at Buntingsdale Hall, Market Drayton, Shropshire.

A new role for Bentley Priory

As part of the RAF's reorganisation into 'role Commands', Fighter Command came into being at Bentley Priory on 14 July 1936, under its Air Officer Commanding-in-Chief (AOC-in-C), Air Marshal Sir Hugh Caswell Tremenheere Dowding KCB, a former Royal Flying Corps officer who had begun his career in 1900 in the Royal Garrison Artillery. Nicknamed 'Stuffy' due to his somewhat stern and austere manner and way of life, Dowding was a teetotal vegetarian who loved bird-watching and dabbled in spiritualism. A strong character, he had commanded Fighting Area in 1929/30 during the earlier Air Defence of Great Britain period and subsequently had served for several years on the Air Council as the Air Member for Research & Development. When he arrived at Bentley Priory at precisely 09.00 hours on 14 July, Dowding was admitted by a zealous security guard, and was then shown round the Station by Sgt. Cornthwaite, the NCO in charge of the

A portrait of Sir Hugh Dowding which typifies his outwardly stern demeanour. His devotion to duty and sheer hard work was, however, a major factor in winning the Battle of Britain.[Crown Copyright via RAF Bentley Priory]

RAF BENTLEY PRIORY AND STANMORE PARK

A pair of Gloster Gamecocks of 23 Squadron; closest to the camera is J7914, which crashed at RAF Sutton bridge in 1929. [P.H.T. Green Collection]

orderly room, in the absence of the Camp Commandant.

Dowding's primary and highly important task was to set up at Bentley Priory a Command Operations Room from which Fighter Command's activities in any future conflict could be controlled, with the aid of the rapidly-developing and highly secret Range & Direction Finding system (RDF), later known as radar. A practical control and reporting system also had to be evolved so that movements of enemy aircraft could be displayed on a table in the operations room. To this end, Dowding had attended a meeting as early as 10 June to determine the specification for the room and the vital communications links. A firm champion of the benefits of RDF, Dowding foresaw operations rooms at Group and sector level receiving raid information from RDF Stations and Observer Corps posts, while at Fighter Command HQ additional sources such as intercepted radio messages and the secret service would be received. Group and Sector operations rooms would deal only with the situation in their own areas, while the Command operations room would have a less detailed but comprehensive overview. All information would be used on a two-way basis so that no factors would be overlooked. The concept of 'filtering' radar plots to avoid confusion was the brainchild of Sqn. Ldr. R. G. Hart, who had been given the task of advising Fighter Command on the training of personnel to operate the new RDF system.

The matter of the Fighter Command operations room table then came under discussion. Dowding wished to install and evaluate an experimental table, and wrote to Air Ministry on 2 July asking for permission. He stated in his letter that *"...the ballroom appears to be most suitable for the purpose although this of course may not be desirable as a permanent location owing to the fact that the Priory is extremely conspicuous from the air and the rooms would be very difficult to render gas-proof. I do, however, wish to make a start immediately... ...only by immediate experiment can be determined the requirements necessary for the purpose".*

Occupying most of the former ballroom, the table would be marked by a map covering the area from Edinburgh to the French coast at Cherbourg and from the Welsh border to the Belgian/German border. Along the north and west sides of the room a high-level gallery would be needed for observation purposes. Movements of hostile fighters and bombers as displayed on Group operations tables would be 'told' by telephone to Bentley Priory, where the up-to-date national situation would be set out on the Fighter Command table. Movements of RAF bomber aircraft would also be displayed.

THE ROYAL AIR FORCE ARRIVES

Any information arriving from intelligence sources would come direct to Bentley Priory for onward transmission to Group operations rooms if pertinent. The estimated cost of the experiment was the princely sum of £55, which was approved within three weeks, allowing work to proceed.

To assist him, Dowding had as SASO Air Cdre. A. D. Cunningham CBE, while in charge of administration was Air Cdre. N. J. Gill CB CBE MC. Units directly administered by HQ Fighter Command were 11 (Fighter) Group, with headquarters at Uxbridge and Air Marshal P. B. Joubert de la Ferté CB CMG DSO as its AOC; 22 (Army Cooperation) Group at Farnborough, commanded by Air Cdre. B. E. Sutton DSO OBE MC; and the Observer Corps, under Air Cdre. A. D. Warrington-Morris CMG OBE. The staff establishment allowed for 26 officers, 71 NCOs and other ranks, 20 Observer Corps personnel and 64 civilians, all of whom could be accommodated comfortably. Even the 'other ranks' had a bedroom each. Normal dress for the officers was civilian, except when they were due to go on a staff visit, when they wore uniform. Many of them had seen service in the First World War, and almost all were pilots of the General Duties Branch, who were obliged to fly a certain number of hours each year.

No sooner had Fighter Command become established at Bentley Priory than a large-scale exercise was held from 27 to 30 July. Covering the south and south-eastern portions of the London area, the exercise was designed to provide training for the army's 1st AA Division and the Observer Corps and to test the operational efficiency of 11 Group squadrons. Although the weather was not at its summer best, valuable experience was gained.

Re-armament of the RAF continued apace, many new airfields opening and new squadrons and training establishments coming into being. In Fighter Command, Catterick airfield opened on 5 August 1936, while 151 Squadron was formed on 4 August at North Weald and 46 Squadron at Kenley on 3 September, both equipped with biplane Gloster Gauntlets. The RAF Balloon Centre at Rollestone Camp on Salisbury Plain, however, transferred out of Fighter Command on 1 November and into Training Command, while next day the Meteorological Flight, hitherto based at Duxford, was placed under Bomber Command control at Mildenhall. Four more squadrons swelled Fighter Command's ranks on 1 December when 24, 600, 601 and 604 Squadrons, all based at Hendon, were transferred to 11 Group of Fighter Command, 24 Sqn. being the RAF's major communications unit and the other squadrons, which were units of the AuxAF, flying Demons, Harts and Demons respectively. The final event of the year was the opening of the new airfield at Odiham on 31 December in 22 Group.

As soon as he had become AOC-in-C of Fighter Command, AM Dowding took over from AM Joubert de la Ferté as Chairman of the Home Defence Committee's Sub-Committee on the Reorientation of the Air Defence of Great Britain, a cumbersome title for a group of men dedicated to their task. The first meeting under Dowding's chairmanship was on 29 October 1936, when the Minister for Co-ordination of Defence, Sir Thomas Inskip, asked the members to submit a report on an air defence system to become operational in 1939, without considering the cost. At the time, fighter strength totalled fourteen squadrons of regulars and three Auxiliary Air Force squadrons. The draft Report on an Ideal Air Defence System, produced without delay, amounted to only twelve pages but listed all types of defences, including fighter aircraft, barrage balloons, anti-aircraft guns, and searchlights. Strangely, the Air Ministry, the opinions of which had been sought by the Sub-Committee, opined that a large increase in defensive fighter squadrons might impede the development of offensive bomber strength. War Office and Admiralty representatives on the Sub-Committee were, paradoxically, in favour of substantial fighter expansion, considering that a counter-offensive would not be

One of the most beautiful biplane fighters ever built was the Hawker Fury. They eventually found their way from Squadron to training unit use, as K3730 used by 2FTS. [P.H.T.Green Collection]

effective in the short term. They also believed, correctly as it turned out, that a 'knock-out' attack on London was a distinct likelihood, and therefore many more fighters would be required.

Construction of the experimental operations room went ahead meanwhile, and on 11 December Dowding was in a position to ask Air Ministry for telephone lines to be installed. He also stated that initially the new room would be linked only with 11 Group in order to concentrate minds on development of a fully operational system.

Air Marshal Dowding was promoted to Air Chief Marshal on 1 January 1937, and three days later Sqn. Ldr. C. S. Riccard was appointed as Camp Commandant in place of Sqn. Ldr. J. F. Barrett DSO DFC, who was posted overseas. At the same time, Air Cdre. Gill was placed on the retired list, and was superseded by Air Cdre. A. C. Maund CBE DSO on 28 January.

The Air Ministry's two-year programme to treble the strength of the RAF was well on the way to completion by early 1937, although more fighter squadrons were still coming into being during the early months of that year. At Northolt on 8 March 213 Sqn. formed to fly the obsolescent Gauntlet biplane and 80 Sqn. formed at Kenley, similarly equipped. A week later 73 Sqn. was formed at Mildenhall and 87 Sqn. at Tangmere, both with Hawker Furies, another outdated type. Another seven days saw the formation of 79 Sqn. at Biggin Hill, another Gauntlet-equipped unit. More barrage balloon potential was added by the birth on 17 March of 30 (Barrage Balloon) Group within Fighter Command, with Air Cdre. J. G. Hearson CB CBE DSO (Retd.) as its AOC. For the time being the new Group was accommodated at Tavistock Place in London.

To handle some of the rapidly-growing number of fighter squadrons, 12 (Fighter) Group was formed on 1 April 1937 under the temporary command of Air Cdre. J. H. Tyssen MC. Initially this Group was based at Uxbridge, but moved on 19 May to Hucknall in Nottinghamshire, the better to control its allocated units. New airfields were also steadily coming into being; Church Fenton, Yorkshire, in 12 Group and Debden, Essex, in 11 Group both opened in the latter half of April 1937. On 5 May two AuxAF squadrons, 607 at Usworth and 608 at Thornaby, transferred from 6 (Auxiliary) Group of Bomber Command to 12 Group, Fighter Command as part of the effort to build up fighter

THE ROYAL AIR FORCE ARRIVES

defences of northern England. Three more AuxAF fighter squadrons were formed on 1 June - 612 at Aberdeen (Dyce), 614 at Cardiff (Pengam Moors) and 615 at Kenley.

Hectic expansion notwithstanding, time was found on 26 June 1937 for Fighter Command to take part in the 18th RAF Display at Hendon. Indeed, ACM Dowding was Chairman of the Flying Committee set up for the event, while the AOC of 11 Group controlled the flying programme. That same day, Dowding was awarded the GCVO to add to his decorations. Another event in which Fighter Command participated that summer was the International Air Meeting in Switzerland. The Hawker Furies of 1 Squadron took off from their base at Tangmere on 28 July and after refuelling at Paris (Le Bourget) and Dijon arrived at Zurich. There they gave a demonstration of aerobatics three times before flying back to Tangmere on 3 August. It was at this event that the Messerschmitt Bf.109, the fighter aircraft which only three years later was Fighter Command's adversary, was exhibited, making a considerable impact on the aviation world. In fact one of them won the circuit of the Alps race, another the climb-and-dive competition, a third won the speed event and two more the team race.

Proof, if any were needed, that the infant Luftwaffe was a force to be reckoned with.

The Furies of 1 Sqn. had not been home more than a few days before being one of nineteen squadrons taking part in the annual Home Defence Air Exercises between 9 and 12 August. Afterwards it was reported that 'most day and night raiders were intercepted and attacked', though in view of the lack of modern facilities available to the pilots this seems to have been a somewhat rash claim.

'Chain Home' radar stations operational

By August 1937, trials with RDF were well advanced and three coastal radar stations, at Orfordness, Bawdsey Manor and Canewdon, were in operation and two more were under construction. In an attempt to hide their true purpose, all these sites were known as AMES (Air Ministry Experimental Stations). It was quickly decided that a further fifteen such RDF Stations would be built to complete the chain, known as Chain Home (CH), at

Ground-based Range and Direction Finding - RDF, otherwise known as Radar - was operated as a number of Chain Home (CH) stations around the East and South coasts of Great Britain. These were massive towers, and could be seen from miles away - all reported to RAF Bentley Priory. [Simon Peters collection]

RAF BENTLEY PRIORY AND STANMORE PARK

K5210, a Hawker Audax, one variant of the Hawker Hind family of fighter/trainers. [P.H.T. Green Collection]

a total cost of £1,305,000. Each station consisted of four receiver masts 250 feet (76.2m.) high and four transmitter masts 350 feet (106.7m.) high, the number of masts providing some security in the event of damage by the enemy or by any other factor. The operating radius of each station overlapped that of its neighbours. Detection of aircraft would, it was anticipated, be made within the following parameters:

83 miles at 13,000 feet (134km. at 3963m.)
50 miles at 5000 feet (80km. at 1524m.)
35 miles at 2000 feet (56km. at 610m.)
25 miles at 1000 feet (40km. at 305m.)

Chain Home stations used a frequency of 22 to 30 MHz on wavelengths of 10 to 13.5 metres and had a range of 120 miles (193km.). By the end of November 1937, the Bentley Priory operations room was receiving information on aircraft movements from Bawdsey Manor, from where the same material was being passed to 11 Group at Uxbridge and the Biggin Hill Sector HQ.

Very surprisingly in view of the degree of security which shrouded the RDF project, three senior Luftwaffe officers, Generals Milch, Stumpff and Udet, were allowed to visit Bentley Priory in October 1937 during a tour which also took in other sensitive RAF Stations such as Mildenhall. At lunch in the Priory with the AOC-in-C, Gen. Milch is reported to have said *"Now, gentlemen, let us all be frank! How are you getting on with your experiments in the radio-detection of aircraft approaching your shores?"* At this, confusion reigned! Milch went on to say that he knew about the British RDF system, but future events showed that he had underestimated the advances made and, even more significantly, the way in which the system was be used. These German officers claimed that the Luftwaffe's work on the same subject had put Germany further ahead, an assertion that proved very wrong.

RAF Digby came back into the fighter world on 7 September 1937, when it was transferred from Training Command to 11 Group of Fighter Command. On 8 October 30 (Balloon) Group moved from Tavistock Place to Kelvin House in Cleveland Square, London W1, where after a year it

THE ROYAL AIR FORCE ARRIVES

would develop further.

A tradition of involvement by RAF Bentley Priory in local affairs began on 11 November 1937, when all personnel who could be spared took part in the Armistice Day parade, embellished by two trumpeters from RAF Halton. On the same day, one officer and four NCOs from Bentley Priory laid a wreath on the war memorial at Bushey Heath.

By far the most significant event of this late prewar period, however, took place on 7 December 1937, when 111 Sqn. at Northolt began to re-equip with the new Hawker Hurricane, the first monoplane fighter to enter service with the RAF. Realised by those who knew the true situation, this event was to have far-reaching effects on a conflict which many now saw as inevitable.

With nervous eyes being cast towards the ever-increasing German threat, the Air Ministry became concerned about the security of the experimental operations room at Bentley Priory, which had been in use for about eighteen months. Sites for the operations rooms at 11, 12 and 13 Group Headquarters were selected by May 1938, and early in June the Deputy Director of Plans at the Air Ministry recommended that by March 1939 they should all be underground, as should the Fighter Command room at Bentley Priory. There, modifications were still being made to the experimental layout, a factor which caused ACM Dowding to ask for a decision to be delayed until after the Home Defence Exercises to be held in August.

Before this, several other exercises were staged to test the air defences. On 10 June a mobilisation exercise was held at RAF Hornchurch, with the local fighter squadrons operating by day and night. Between 2 and 7 July a Combined Operations exercise took place, and from 20 to 22 July a Coast Defence exercise was held. In this, the Bentley Priory and 11 Group operations rooms were manned, allowing the RDF organisation to be evaluated. At the end of July the home defence organisation - ARP and air-raid warning arrangements - was tested.

During 1938 the headquarters of the Observer Corps moved from Uxbridge to Bentley Priory. Commandant of the Observer Corps was Air Cdre. A. P. Warrington-Morris CMG OBE RAF (Retd.), who had held the post since 1936 and had presided over a rapid and continuing expansion in line with the growth of the RAF. By the end of August 1938 twenty Groups of the Observer Corps had been formed, each controlling a large number of Posts, many of them in isolated country districts, manned by volunteers drawn from all walks of life. Their task was a vital one — that of supplementing the information provided by the coastal RDF Stations, which could not plot the inland flight of an aircraft. At this stage the Posts were not manned on a full-time basis, but training interspersed with regular exercises was carried out.

The Spitfire in service
Deliveries of Fighter Command's second monoplane fighter type, the Supermarine Spitfire, began on 28 July 1938, 19 Squadron at Duxford being the first recipient. This type was, of course, destined to become the public's favourite fighter in the Battle of Britain, although the Hurricane was much more numerous and achieved better numerical results.

The important Home Defence exercises were held over the first weekend of August 1938 and demonstrated that the RDF system functioned well, although the RAF plotters at Bawdsey Manor were not as experienced as the civilian scientists who had brought the system to its current stage. It was found that the High Frequency (HF) radio carried by the fighter aircraft lacked sufficient range, and there was thus a demand for more forward direction-finding stations. Another urgent need was for the installation of more IFF (Identification: Friend or Foe) equipment in British aircraft. An outcome of the exercises was the decision that the complete filter organisation would be moved from Bawdsey Manor to Bentley Priory. To boost the Priory staff for the duration of the exercise, 37 extra airmen

RAF BENTLEY PRIORY AND STANMORE PARK

Spitfire Mk.I K9851, of 19 Sqdn.

were attached from 2 to 8 August to work in the operations room, making a continuous watch possible. These men lived under canvas in the Priory grounds during their stay. Visitors to the operations room during the exercise included the War Minister, Mr. Hore-Belisha, accompanied by Maj. Gen. Hill, and Col. H. L. Ismay.

The Munich crisis
As far back as 24 March 1938, the Prime Minister, Neville Chamberlain, had warned Germany that Britain was ready to go to war to defend France and Belgium against unprovoked attack, although we would not automatically protect Czechoslovakia. On 31 August, the British Ambassador to Berlin, Sir Neville Henderson, was recalled for consultations after Germany had begun to take a threatening posture against Czechoslovakia, and Sir John Simons, the Chancellor of the Exchequer, reiterated Chamberlain's statement. Bentley Priory personnel were recalled from leave late on 25 September, and next day the Command, Group and Sector operations rooms were manned with skeleton staffs and the air raid warning system was tested. The crisis developed rapidly. At 14.30 on 26 September the filter room at Bawdsey Manor began to operate a continuous watch, and at 15.40 the Air Ministry ordered the Observer Corps to be called out. Half an hour later the army's Home Defence scheme became operative. At 16.30 a message was sent from Bentley Priory to the three Fighter Groups ordering them to man their operations rooms, and Bentley Priory's own operations room came into full use at 18.00. The Auxiliary Air Force was embodied at 19.45, and at the same time the balloon barrages were ordered to deploy to war sites but not to inflate the balloons. Next day the Air Ministry stated that all airfields were being camouflaged and that fighter aircraft were to have code letters painted on their fuselages to identify the squadrons with which they were serving.

As part of the precautions, a large air exercise involving 945 aircraft was held on 28 September to give practice to AA and searchlight units around London. A mass bomber attack was made by 36 squadrons of bombers (the 'Eastland' force) on 'Westland', which was defended by 23 fighter squadrons guided by RDF, and the BBC and the press were kept informed. Next day four AuxAF fighter squadrons were placed on war status and exercises were held by 11 and 12 Groups. On 30 September 11 Group aircraft flying without navigation lights provided further practice for Territorial Army searchlight crews around London. A visitor to the

THE ROYAL AIR FORCE ARRIVES

A line of new Hawker Hurricane Mk.Is at RAF Northolt in July 1938, with the pilots gathered for a posed publicity picture.
[via Alistair Goodrum]

Bentley Priory operations room that day was the Air Minister, Sir Kingsley Wood. Taking part in this exercise was the Observer Corps, the men of which manned their Posts from 26 September until being stood down on 1 October.

Neville Chamberlain, meanwhile, had gone to Munich with a peace plan, and on 30 September announced that an agreement on a peaceful solution of the Czech crisis had been signed by Hitler, Mussolini, Daladier and himself. *"I believe it is peace for our time"*, he said optimistically on arriving at Heston Airport. Tension then eased, and all units reverted to normal duties at 13.00 on 1 October, although no weekend leave was allowed. Less than a week later the German army invaded Czech Sudetenland. Although the Munich agreement was an example of appeasement, it did give Great Britain a further eleven months of extremely valuable time in which to continue rearmament.

When the crisis was over, the Air Ministry ordered all the AuxAF fighter squadrons to remain embodied at their home Stations. Barrage balloons not already withdrawn would remain deployed, the remainder to be ready for movement to war sites within twelve hours. The RAF in general was to stay at 'readiness', but leave could be granted subject to recall at short notice.

RAF BENTLEY PRIORY AND STANMORE PARK

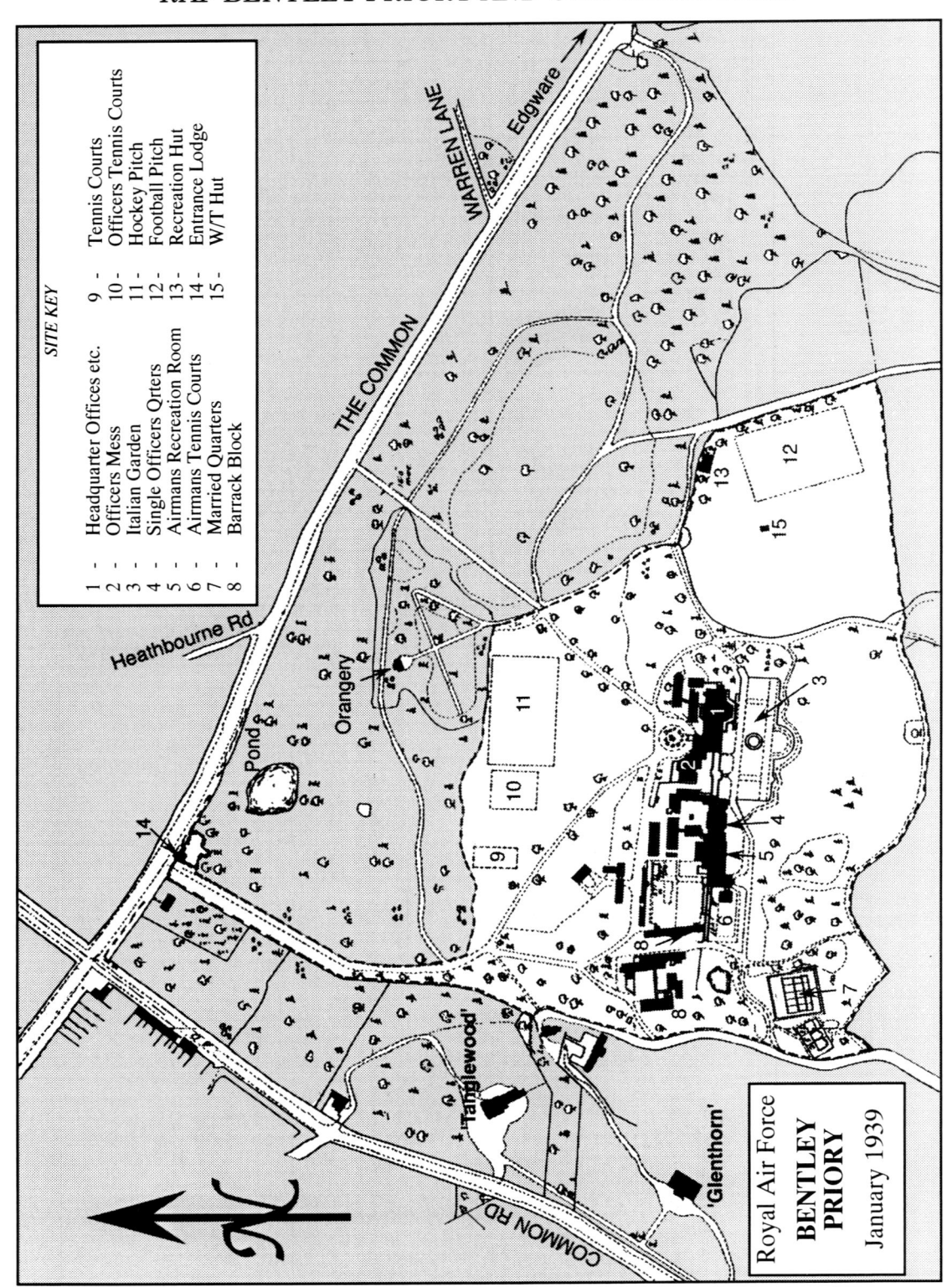

SITE KEY

1 - Headquarter Offices etc.
2 - Officers Mess
3 - Italian Garden
4 - Single Officers Qrters
5 - Airmans Recreation Room
6 - Airmans Tennis Courts
7 - Married Quarters
8 - Barrack Block
9 - Tennis Courts
10 - Officers Tennis Courts
11 - Hockey Pitch
12 - Football Pitch
13 - Recreation Hut
14 - Entrance Lodge
15 - W/T Hut

Royal Air Force
BENTLEY PRIORY
January 1939

THE ROYAL AIR FORCE ARRIVES

Recruitment into the RAF had been stimulated by recent events and by a favourable press reaction. This lead to the first member of the RAF Volunteer Reserve (RAFVR) enlisting on 25 October for duty in the operations room at the Priory, where fifteen airmen had arrived on 3 October for intelligence duties.

Operations to move underground

Probably given extra impetus by the Munich crisis, the decision to build an underground operations room at Bentley Priory was confirmed on 25 September 1938. The work was estimated to cost £45,000, and hutted accommodation for the necessary extra staff was also planned. Apart from this project, it was now absolutely clear that Bentley Priory would see considerable growth within the next few months, and building and alteration work was speeded up. New offices for the 1st AA Corps, the AMWD Chief Engineer and certain HQ staff were brought into use on 28 October 1938, although other AMWD personnel moved to Valency House at Northwood at the same time. Most significantly, the temporary filter room was completed and on 8 November assumed control of the RDF organisation from Bawdsey Manor, from where experienced staff were transferred. This filter room was in the safety of the basement at Bentley Priory, and had previously seen service as an office and general store. On the domestic front, a new sergeants' mess came into use on 26 November.

A third monoplane aircraft type, the twin-engined Bristol Blenheim, entered service with Fighter Command as a night-fighter on 5 December 1938, when the first example joined 23 Squadron at Wittering. Once crews had been trained on this modern machine, the air defence capability of the RAF was raised considerably. Impetus was added to the rearmament programme on 6 December 1938, when France and Germany signed a pact confirming the inviolability of their joint frontier, an agreement which in Britain was widely considered to be nothing more than a threatening ploy on the part of Germany.

Work on the underground operations complex, scheduled originally for completion in September 1939, proceeded slowly. From January 1939 the work went on round the clock, seventy men being employed during daylight hours and twenty-five at night. Delays were caused during the construction period when the specification was altered to provide for a greater degree of protection, the criterion now being that a direct hit by a 500lb (227kg.) bomb or a 250lb. (113kg.) semi-armour-piercing bomb should be withstood. Excavation averaged a depth of 42 feet (12.8m.) and 58,270 tons of earth were dug out. Concrete poured totalled 23,500 tons, and a huge amount of steel reinforcement was used. Further delays occurred when it was found that dampness might cause corrosion in communications cables.

Fighter Command's disposition on 1 January 1939 comprised three Groups — 11 (Fighter) Group at Uxbridge, 12 (Fighter) Group at Hucknall and 22 (Army Cooperation) Group at Farnborough. 11 Group was in the process of re-equipping with Hurricanes, of which eight squadrons were fully equipped and one partly, and Spitfires, of which there was so far just one squadron. Three squadrons of Blenheim twin-engined fighters were included, but there were still three squadrons of obsolescent Gladiator biplanes and two of Gauntlets. Further north, 12 Group was much less well equipped, with two squadrons of Spitfires, one of Hurricanes and one of Blenheims, the remainder of the inventory being Gladiators, Gauntlets, Hinds and Demons. For army cooperation purposes, 22 Group flew Hector and Hind biplanes and Lysander aircraft, which were very useful in forward battle situations.

A new Private Branch Exchange came into use at Bentley Priory on 1 January 1939, aiding communications between Fighter Command HQ staff and the ever-growing number of squadrons and fighter airfields. Even though work was proceeding on the beefed-up underground operations room, the Air Ministry in February 1939 discussed with the GPO the possible siting of a standby for use in the event of the temporary facilities at Bentley Priory being destroyed or severely damaged by enemy action. The outcome was that an emergency operations room with a secondary task as a training centre for operations staff was established in July 1939 at Liscombe Park, near Leighton Buzzard.

Another long-term resident, albeit an army organisation, AA Command was formed at RAF Bentley Priory on 1 April 1939 under the command of General Brooke, although he left on 28 July to take command of the British Expeditionary Forces and was replaced by Gen. Sir Frederick Pile. AA Command headquarters from July 1939 were at *'Glenthorn'*, a large house with access from Common Road, within easy walking distance of the Priory and thus convenient for open-air meetings between Gen. Pile and ACM Dowding, who lived with his sister Hilda at a house, no longer in existence, called *'Montrose'* in Gordon Avenue, Stanmore. *'Glenthorn'* had been the home of Mr. Frederick Gordon of Gordon's Hotels, whose family crest became the badge of AA Command.

The monthly home defence exercise held on 4 April 1939 was notable in the number of visitors to Bentley Priory it attracted, among them AVM Williams and Gp. Capt. Macnamara of the Royal Australian Air Force, Col. van der Spuy of the South African Air Force, Sqn. Ldr. Heakes of the Royal Canadian Air Force and two Australian scientists, all no doubt keen on seeing at first hand the RDF system in operation. Three weeks later, officers of a French mission came to see what was happening in the operations room. Most significant, however, as later events would show, was the visit on 1 June of Winston Churchill MP, who at that time was still in the political wilderness.

Pending the opening of the underground facilities, the filtering function established only recently in the Bentley Priory basement was moved upstairs on 20 May 1939 to less safe but more practical surroundings next to the operations room. There, a balcony supported by timber framework was built so that the map table below could be seen to advantage. A gap was knocked through the ornate wall into the operations room next door so that staff could move freely between the two rooms. During 1939 the large conservatory was removed and wooden huts for use as offices by the operations staff were erected in its place. Other measures included the camouflaging of the hitherto white Priory building with green and brown paint, the protection of some buildings by sandbags and the building of dug-out shelters, while a number of trees were cut back to allow a better field of fire in the event of an invasion.

Achtung Zeppelin!

Late in May 1939, RDF stations on the east coast picked up a strong radar response from a large slow-moving object over the North Sea. The echo turned out to be the German airship LZ130 *Graf Zeppelin,* which was carrying Gen. Wolfgang Martini, the Luftwaffe's Chief of Signals, on a mission to investigate the British radar defence system. Flying in cloud, the airship blatantly reported its position off the Yorkshire coast by radio to its German base. The idea of contacting the *Graf Zeppelin* to issue a correction, as it was really several miles inland over Hull, was considered but rejected, as this would have confirmed that the airship was indeed being watched, a fact which was best kept secret. A further flight was made by the *Graf Zeppelin* in August but was not seen by the RDF stations.

In the control tower at Croydon Airport at this time was a telephone labelled 'secret', with direct connection to the Operations Room at Bentley Priory. The duty controller at Croydon became accustomed to receiving calls from Bentley Priory asking him, for example, *"Has an aircraft bound for you recently taken off from Paris?"*. To this he would reply *"Yes,*

THE ROYAL AIR FORCE ARRIVES

it's now flying over the French coast at 4000 feet". The reply from the Priory was likely to be *"Yes, that's right!"*, which intrigued the Croydon staff, who had heard vague whisperings about a new 'magic' detection system. Later, when several of the Croydon Airport controllers headed by pioneer controller Jimmy Jeffs were seconded to Bentley Priory to act as civilian liaison officers they saw at first hand the effectiveness of RDF and how airliners could be diverted to avoid bad weather. They also saw how inaccurate some visual position reports were!

War imminent

The prospect of war loomed ever larger on the horizon during the summer of 1939. A home defence exercise carried out between 8 and 11 August turned out to be the final one, and the last chance to test the RDF system, which by then was in operation around the coast between Bawdsey Manor and Dover. ACM Dowding, expressing his thoughts on the subject, said *"The system worked extremely well, and although doubtless capable of improvements as a result of experience, may now be said to have settled down to an acceptable standard"*.

A system of intelligence-gathering and dissemination was, however, still lacking. This exercise also gave the Observer Corps valuable further experience. At each Observer Corps Centre, information was received from up to 36 Posts and then 'told' to the appropriate fighter sectors. Members of the Corps at Post level were not, however, allowed to know anything about the RDF system, which remained highly secret. Scientists were allocated to each Centre to make confidential checks on the coordination of RDF and Observer Corps plots and then to analyse the results of the exercise fully.

At this time of extreme tension, messages flooding into and out of Bentley Priory gave instructions and information on the minute-by-minute situation. Examples taken from the Fighter Command main Operations Record Book, with remarks added by the author, are:

22 August Fighter Command instructed 25 Squadron to move to its war station next day. [This squadron was equipped with Blenheim aircraft, and moved from RAF Hawkinge to RAF Northolt as ordered].

23 August (01.26) Air Ministry ordered 500, 501, 502, 504, 600 - 605, 607 - 616, 911 - 947 Squadrons to prepare in secrecy as a precautionary measure notices calling out all Auxiliary Air Force personnel. [The 500 and 600 series units were Reserve and AuxAF fighter squadrons and the 900 series were balloon squadrons].

23 August (10.47) Air Ministry ordered immediate formation of Personnel Transit Centres.

23 August (11.41) Air Ministry ordered immediate formation of Nos. 1 to 4 Air Ammunition Parks.

23 August (15.12) Air Ministry ordered whole of Auxiliary Air Force to be called up.

23 August (15.34) Air Ministry instructed that all key men be recalled from leave immediately.

23 August (21.56) Air Ministry instructed all units that Class E reservists and up to 3000 RAFVR were to be called up. Advanced Air Striking Force to mobilise for France but remain in place for the time being.

23 August (22.26) Fighter Command informed 501, 605, 609, 613, 614 and 616 Sqns. that Army Home Defence Scheme was to be put into force on 25 August.

24 August (00.25) Air Ministry informed Fighter Command and Balloon Command that London balloon barrage be deployed to war sites on 25 August but not inflated.

24 August (00.35) Air Ministry cancelled last order.

24 August (12.00) Fighter Command

THE ROYAL AIR FORCE ARRIVES

instructed to report when mobilisation complete and 504, 600, 601, 604, 605, 608, 610, 611 and 615 Squadrons ready to move to war status.

24 August (13.05) Croydon [Airport] not to be operational.

24 August (15.45) Fighter Command instructed all Stations that instructions for camouflage were to be put in hand as soon as possible.

24 August (18.06) Air Ministry sent action code message "ACTION AOGAYOR".

24 August (20.32) Air Ministry instructed Fighter Command and Balloon Command that provincial barrages were to be deployed commencing 25 August but not inflated.

24 August (21.06) All personnel on leave from all units to be recalled, without any publicity. AA Command ordered the full manning of gun and searchlight posts.

25 August (02.28) Air Ministry instructed Fighter Command to recall all personnel of Bawdsey Research Station on leave.

26 August (12.59) Air Ministry instructed Balloon Command to inflate London and provincial barrages but not to fly above 100 feet.

Fourteen minutes after receiving the action message on 24 August, the Chief Signals Officer, Wg. Cdr. I. M. Rodney, telephoned the Chief Trunk Supervisor at the London Trunk Exchange and passed code word ARMADILLO, which activated the switching of air defence and anti-aircraft landline circuits by 20.30 hours. He also sent the following message to Chief Constables and to the officers of all Observer Corps Groups: "EMPOL Section eleven Observer Corps readiness at 20.30 hours on 24.8.39. Acknowledge to AIRGENARCH STANMORE". Within two hours about twenty thousand men of the Observer Corps had reported for duty and the GPO had switched 2330 circuits to wartime function, involving 4940 switching routes, both quite amazing feats of organisation. The Observer Corps remained 'on watch' from that night until the end of hostilities in 1945!

General mobilisation

General mobilisation of the RAF was promulgated on 1 September, blackout orders were issued and stricter precautions against intruders were taken, involving the issue of identity passes with photographs. At Bentley Priory, the 32nd and 247th AA Battalions and the 2nd West Kent Regt. took up defensive positions. The first civilian building requisitioned locally was the Bushey Heath Children's Convalescent Home, which was taken over on 1 September as a 17-bed Station Sick Quarters.

On the same day inflation of the London balloon barrage was completed. Some difficulty was experienced with balloons which broke from their moorings in bad weather, one of which drifted over East Ham and had to be shot down by a fighter from North Weald.

War on Germany was declared by Great Britain and France at 11.00 on 3 September 1939, and the Prime Minister appointed Winston Churchill to be First Lord of the Admiralty, a position he had held at the beginning of the First World War. Aware that the safety of the underground operations room was not yet available, the staff of Fighter Command at RAF Bentley Priory awaited events, probably with trepidation. Under the Command's control were 38 front-line squadrons — seventeen flying Hurricanes, eleven with Spitfires, seven with Blenheims, two with obsolete Gladiator biplanes and one on the point of re-equipping from Gauntlets and Battles to Spitfires. Three of the six Hurricane squadrons in 12 Group would leave in a matter of days to go to France as part of the Advanced Air Striking Force, depleting Fighter Command's defensive capacity in the Midlands area. The question on the nation's collective mind now was whether Great Britain would be invaded in the same way as other European countries.

RAF BENTLEY PRIORY AND STANMORE PARK

Chapter Three

The War Years

The time will come when thou shalt lift thine eyes
To watch a long-drawn battle in the skies
While aged peasants, too amazed for words,
Stare at the flying fleets of wond'rous birds.
England, so long mistress of the sea,
Where winds and waves confess her sovereignty,
Her ancient triumphs yet on high shall bear,
And reign, the sovereign of the conquered air.

(Translated from Gray's 'Luna Habitabilis'; Cambridge, 1797)

The outbreak of the Second World War was announced on BBC radio by the Prime Minister, Rt. Hon. Neville Chamberlain, at 11.00 on 3 September 1939, and within fifteen minutes the air raid sirens could be heard in and around London. This turned out to be a false alarm, the result of mis-identification of aircraft flying from France. Steps were quickly taken to improve the defences of Bentley Priory by erecting barbed wire fences, and walls of sandbags were built as protection to vulnerable buildings and gun sites. Windows were painted with black paint and the Priory building itself was painted dull green.

With the influx of personnel, many of whom were now working on a shift basis, overcrowding became inevitable. Requisitioning of local properties to help alleviate this problem began as soon as war had been declared. *'County End'* in Magpie Hall Road, Bushey, was taken over as officers' quarters on 3 September, and Tanglewood School became billets for personnel of the West Kent Regt. at the same time. Next day, Nos. 1 and 3 Hartsbourne Road were occupied by ATS girls. On 5 September orders were issued for RAF married quarters to be vacated so that the Fighter Command HQ Unit could be established. During the rest of the month more buildings were requisitioned - appropriately-named *'Ad Astra'* in Priory Drive became offices for the 247th Battalion AA and *'Barlogan'*, in the same road, was occupied by WAAF and ATS officers as their mess on 11 September; the ATS took over *'Bushmead'* in California Lane and 'Elderslie' in Magpie Hall Road became No.2 Officers' Mess on 17 September; and 'Rosary Priory' in Elstree Road was taken over as WAAF hostel next day. At the same time, siting for hutted accommodation in the Bentley Priory grounds began.

To see at first hand the very serious situation in which the United Kingdom found itself, HM King George VI visited Bentley Priory on 6 September and was received by ACM Dowding and the C-in-C of the AA defences. The King was shown round the operations room and filter room, where the RDF system was explained to him, and afterwards he visited AA Command and some local gun sites. Earlier that day, at 06.15, there had been a raid warning after AA searchlight crews on Mersea Island, Essex had reported seeing a large number of high-flying aircraft heading toward the Thames Estuary. At this stage neither the RDF Stations nor the Observer Corps posts could confirm that the aircraft were hostile, but at 06.30

RAF BENTLEY PRIORY AND STANMORE PARK

The ornate wallpaper in this picture of the upper gallery of the temporary Operations Room at Bentley Priory in early 1940 is exactly the same as appears in photographs of the Priory when it was a girls school. The map on the wall and the one clipped to the table are divided into numbered areas which were used for air raid warning purposes. The officer working on the table was Gp. Capt. Smallwood. [Crown copyright]

11 Group operations room ordered six Hurricanes of 56 Sqn. at North Weald to 'scramble' and fly a patrol between Harwich and Colchester. In fact all fourteen available pilots of the squadron took to the air in a state of exuberance, without making the North Weald sector controller aware of their increased number. These quickly became confused with the original sightings, and four Flights of Spitfires were ordered into the air to attack what was apparently a hostile formation. Spotting the Hurricanes in silhouette against the sun, the Spitfire pilots attacked. One Hurricane was shot down and its pilot killed, while another pilot survived a crash-landing. Fortunately, the CO of 151 Sqn. realised what was happening and yelled over his R/T "Do not retaliate - bandits are friendly". The incident became known as The Battle of Barking Creek, which was the main sewage outfall for Greater London, not far from Hornchurch, the base of many of the offending Spitfires. Two Spitfire pilots were arrested and charged but acquitted, but the unfortunate sector controller at North Weald, Gp. Capt. D.F. Lucking, was court-martialled for his part in the fiasco, full details of which may never be revealed. It is probable that the original sighting at East Mersea was nothing more than a gaggle of geese making their may to their feeding areas.

On the outbreak of war, the RDF service was operational at eighteen Chain Home stations. Personnel at these sites detected approaching aircraft, their distance, and in reasonable conditions their direction and the height at which

THE WAR YEARS

In this picture of a very crowded temporary Operations Room in the Priory building early in 1940 the plotting table in the well can be seen, with the timber structure supporting the balcony behind it. [Crown copyright]

they were flying. This information was passed by direct telephone line to the filter room at Bentley Priory and thence to Group and Sector, where by plotting reports from two or more RDF Stations the position of the hostile aircraft could be determined. Fighter Command's operations room at Bentley Priory was provided with an overview of the situation, the control of intercepting fighters being handled at Group level. A vital task which was carried out at the Priory, however, was the initiation of air raid warnings throughout the United Kingdom.

Arrival of the WAAF

For the first time, WAAFs took over one daytime watch in the Bentley Priory filter room as plotters on 20 September, after 33 of them had been welcomed by the Director of the WAAF, Air Commandant Katherine J. Trefusis-Forbes. The girls, who had been given two weeks' training in plotting at Leighton Buzzard, naturally soon became objects of great interest to the male population of the room, but it was thought that the WAAFs might not be able to cope with long periods of concentration. Questions were also raised about the possible effects on them of a direct air raid, and it was some time before they were fully accepted. Their billet was at *'The Warren'*, a country house opposite St. Peter's church in Bushey Heath, from where they were carried in a coach to work each day. No complete uniforms were available to the girls, who perforce had to make do with an assortment of garments until such time as supplies of regulation clothing arrived.

Teleprinters were installed to enable information to be passed from Sector and

RAF BENTLEY PRIORY AND STANMORE PARK

Group operations rooms through Air Ministry liaison officers at Bentley Priory to the War Room at Air Ministry. If he needed such confirmation, ACM Dowding received on 20 September a letter from the Air Council stating *"I am to confirm that full operational control of the active air defences of Great Britain, consisting of the Observer Corps, fighter and balloon units of the Royal Air Force and gun and searchlight units of the army, is vested in yourself as AOC-in-C Fighter Command"*. What a load for any pair of shoulders! A further message from Air Ministry, issued on 27 September, informed all Commands that though there had not yet been any raids, a false sense of security should be avoided. September turned out to be, in the words of one officer, *"...a war of alarm rather than excursion"*.

One of the earliest suspicious plots recorded by the CH stations was on 28 September, when it was thought that enemy aircraft were mine-laying in the Thames Estuary.

To assist in dealing with the rapidly-increasing quantity of coded messages, several of the wives of officers serving at Bentley Priory were drafted in and trained to work in this department, and by early October eight of the ladies were busy in a hut at the eastern end of the main building. Working with them were a number of reservists, other civilians and veterans of the First World War, among them ACM Dowding's step-daughter Brenda Vancourt, who later became an officer in the WAAF.

Intense concentration is apparent in this scene in the Filter Room in Bentley Priory early in 1940 - but it also shows the shortages of uniforms; one of the girls on the left is wearing a distinctly civilian skirt! The civilians to the right of the table were probably radar scientists maintaining a watching brief on the operational results of their newly-introduced equipment.
[Crown copyright]

THE WAR YEARS

Fighter Command's first - line equipment on 11 October 1939 amounted to 118 Spitfires, 155 Hurricanes, 82 Blenheims and 47 obsolete Gladiators — hardly a massive battle-fleet! In the House of Commons, Sir Kingsley Wood stated on 25 October that the air defence of the United Kingdom must be controlled by the AOC-in-C of Fighter Command [Dowding], who would exercise his discretion in accordance with a new policy of sounding air raid warnings only when an attack became highly probable.

With Gen. Pile at its head, AA Command controlled guns positioned within a 25-mile (40km.) wide belt stretching from Newcastle down the East coast, around London and south-west to Portsmouth. Included in the belt were 960 searchlights, whose operators were highly vulnerable to attack by enemy aircraft, and the whole system was manned by 23,000 personnel. Also at the Priory was the headquarters of the indefatigable Observer Corps, controlling, by November 1939, 32 Centres, which in turn administered 1000 posts manned by about 25,000 men and women.

Properties taken over

More building requisitions took place as space was needed for the ever-growing numbers of RAF, WAAF and army personnel at Bentley Priory. *'Otway Cottage'* in Elstree Road became another WAAF hostel on 10 October, while the girls of the ATS found themselves using *'Arrochar'* in Hartsbourne Road. On 14 October 78 High Road in Bushey was taken over for WAAF use as a sick quarters. One WAAF who arrived in November 1939, 888601 ACW2 Elizabeth Trouncer, possessed as a uniform only a RAF raincoat and a navy blue beret! She

'Glenthorn' was the home of Frederick Gordon, the owner of Bentley Priory when it was a hotel. During the Second World War 'Glenthorn' was taken over as the headquarters of the army's Anti-Aircraft Command under Gen. Sir Frederick Pile, who found the short walk to Fighter Command headquarters at RAF Bentley Priory beneficial.

RAF BENTLEY PRIORY AND STANMORE PARK

'Montrose' was the large house taken over from its civilian owner for use as the home of the AOC-in-C Fighter Command. Seen here in 1940, it has since been demolished. [Sir Ivor Broom]

recalls that there were infinitely long queues for clothing, including underwear, but eventually each girl had a uniform of sorts. *"We were then paraded"*, she says, *"and were inspected by the Duchess of Gloucester, who asked me why my jacket was a different colour from my skirt, and told me to change it — more queuing! I remember that civilian cleaners were employed; one day an Air Commodore told a woman to get on with it, whereupon she threw down her cloth and shouted 'Clean it yer bloody self'!"*

The girls of the WAAF suffered some privations in their requisitioned billets. *"We had to share a bathroom"* recalls the former ACW Trouncer (now Mrs. Duncan), *"with one girl on the seat, one in the bath and one washing her hair at the basin! There was no privacy at all. I was in a dormitory for nine. The girl next to me was spotlessly clean, and played hockey for Woolworth's on Wednesdays and for Soper's on Saturdays. She had a pen friend who sent her his photograph, but when she went to meet him......he turned out to be only five feet tall! We were a real mixed bag. I queued for my first high tea, and as I got up to the hatch a tough North Country girl [nudged me] with her elbow and sent me reeling across the room. We often found that the RAF high tea, often with dried egg, was inadequate, and so repaired to the YMCA, where for a small sum you could get a real egg and bacon to fill the cracks. They were a blessing"*.

The West Kent Regt. vacated Tanglewood School on 14 October to make way for about ninety RAF men who had been living under canvas. On the main site new barrack hutting began to come into use on 30 October, and on 22 November a 100-seat dining room was completed. A Sick Quarters for WAAF and ATS use was set up in another commandeered building, *'Honduras'* in Bushey High Road on 10 November. ACM Dowding himself lived in a substantial house named *'Montrose'* in Gordon Avenue, Stanmore, with his sister.

An important part of the modernisation

THE WAR YEARS

of the RAF was the provision of VHF radio-telephone (R/T) in front-line aircraft, and in Fighter Command the first machine to be fitted with VHF began its trials at Duxford on 30 October 1939. Barely two weeks later, the HF radios in 66 Squadron's Spitfires at Duxford were replaced by the new equipment, this squadron being the pioneer. Another 'first' at this time was the commissioning of the first Chain Home Low (CHL) station, at Fifeness in Scotland, on 1 November, giving the RDF operators the much-needed ability to detect low-flying aircraft which the CH stations would miss. In order to keep the amount of 'traffic' down to a level which could be handled without a significant increase in filter room staff, each CHL Station was parented by a CH Station through which plots were passed.

Given the sluggishness of events during November 1939, it was generally assumed at Fighter Command HQ that Germany had shelved the idea of an air offensive so that the suspense would have an effect on the morale of the British people: a war of nerves, in fact. That month, the SASO approved a 15% reduction in power at all the RDF stations, subject of course to operational factors, as more of the vital transmitter valves were being used than could be replaced. An emergency operations room near Leighton Buzzard, completed during November, was available for use within one hour for vital communications and could be fully operational within six hours. At Bentley Priory, however, staff continued to work in

Their Majesties King George VI and Queen Elizabeth (the present Queen Mother) visited RAF Bentley Priory on 6 September 1940, and are seen here strolling in the grounds in company with ACM Sir Hugh Dowding, AOC-in-C Fighter Command.
[Crown Copyright via RAF Bentley Priory]

RAF BENTLEY PRIORY AND STANMORE PARK

the temporary operations rooms, where they were visited by the Rt. Hon. Clement R. Attlee MP and Sir Edward Campbell MP on 20 November and by the Prime Minister and the Chief of the Air Staff five days later. In the event of damage by enemy action, headquarters staff would have moved to the premises of the Building Research Station at Garston, near Watford.

Most of the 32nd. Battery Light AA personnel left on 1 December, leaving behind two light guns which were removed two weeks later. *'High Trees'* in London Road, Stanmore, was taken over as accommodation for thirty WAAFs on 11 December, while a further 38 of the girls moved into *'Two Oaks'* in Elstree Road. Yet another contingent of thirty WAAFs found a home in *'Woodham Ferrers'* in Priory Drive. Eventually, three 15-cwt. vans were provided to ferry the girls between hostel and work, but not until late March 1940! Amid all the hectic activity, time was found on 21 December to stage a children's party. More barrack huts were being occupied, as was the guard house, the Code & Cypher hut and the equipment store, which came into use in February 1940. The last of twelve Summers shelters was also brought into use. On the other hand, the garage at *'Glenthorn Lodge'*, the CO's quarters, was burnt out on 17 February and his car destroyed, prompting the setting-up of a Court of Enquiry.

In December 1939 one of the many young men 'called up' was Harold Gross, who since 1936 had worked as a junior civil servant at the Air Ministry, latterly at King Charles St. in London. There he had been responsible for security and the defence of the building in the event of an invasion. By chance, late in 1938 he came into contact with Sqn. Ldr. J. W. Gillan, who on 10 February that year had set a new speed record by flying a Hurricane fighter from Edinburgh to Northolt in 48 minutes at an average speed of 408.75 mph (approx. 658 kph). Gillan mentioned that the RAF was looking for young men to

Those at the sharp end - Bentley Priory may have been at the top of the command structure, but others had to fight. Left: Spitfire IIs of 123 Sqn, with P7443 closest to the camera and below: Hurricane I N2479 of 56 Sqn and personel. [Ray Sturtivant]

THE WAR YEARS

Part of the defence of Great Britain depended on Barrage Balloons, as seen here, used to keep ememy aircraft away from strategic targets.

undertake secret work in the event of hostilities, and Harold Gross readily agreed and was told that he would be sent to Bentley Priory. So in December he found himself at RAF Uxbridge, where he was kitted out and became 912916 AC2 Gross H. V. After three days he was told to travel in civilian clothes to Bentley Priory due to the high degree of secrecy being maintained there. Arriving at Stanmore by train, he found a 142 bus and, in view of the secrecy, whispered to the conductor to tell him when the bus arrived at the Priory. *"You'll know when we get there"* replied the conductor, and sure enough outside the entrance to the Priory there was a large RAF crest telling the world that this was the HQ of Fighter Command! So much for secrecy!

Asked by the service policeman at the guardroom why he was wearing 'civvies', Harold replied *"Because this is a secret Station"* and was told to report to the Orderly Room. There he encountered the Station Warrant Officer, who told him in no uncertain terms to get into uniform. That done, he reported for duty, having undergone no basic training — 'square-bashing' — or instruction in his future work. His job was to be a 'teller' in the Filter Room in the Priory, where he took messages from RDF Stations. Adding to his confusion was the fact that he had to find his own accommodation wherever he could!

One of the supplementary duties carried out by AC2 Gross and others was acting as a bodyguard for ACM Dowding. This task entailed 'standing by' in a picquet room for 24-hour stretches, and if an alarm bell rang hurrying to stand outside Dowding's office, rifle at the ready. Unfortunately, on the first occasion when the alarm was heard (a practice, though the men did not know that) nobody, least of all the corporal in charge, had thought to ask for any ammunition!

By the end of 1939, a fully-integrated air defence network was effectively complete. Fighter Command had at its disposal radar in the shape of the RDF Stations; vital visual observation by the many thousands of members of the Observer Corps; secure operations rooms working in a co-ordinated way; good telephone communications; the Y-Service intelligence network, which included the de-coding of messages passed on the German 'Enigma' code system; and the direction of fighter aircraft by R/T. A supplementary watch was made on enemy aircraft movements by means of reports transmitted by W/T from shipping via the RDF stations, but in February 1940 this route was discontinued and such messages began to arrive at Bentley Priory by other means. At this early stage of the war, the Luftwaffe had few of these advantages, a fact which was to be brought home to the enemy before then end of 1940.

Defence of the realm also depended on the Observer Corps making visual sightings of enemy numbers, position and direction of attack.

RAF BENTLEY PRIORY AND STANMORE PARK

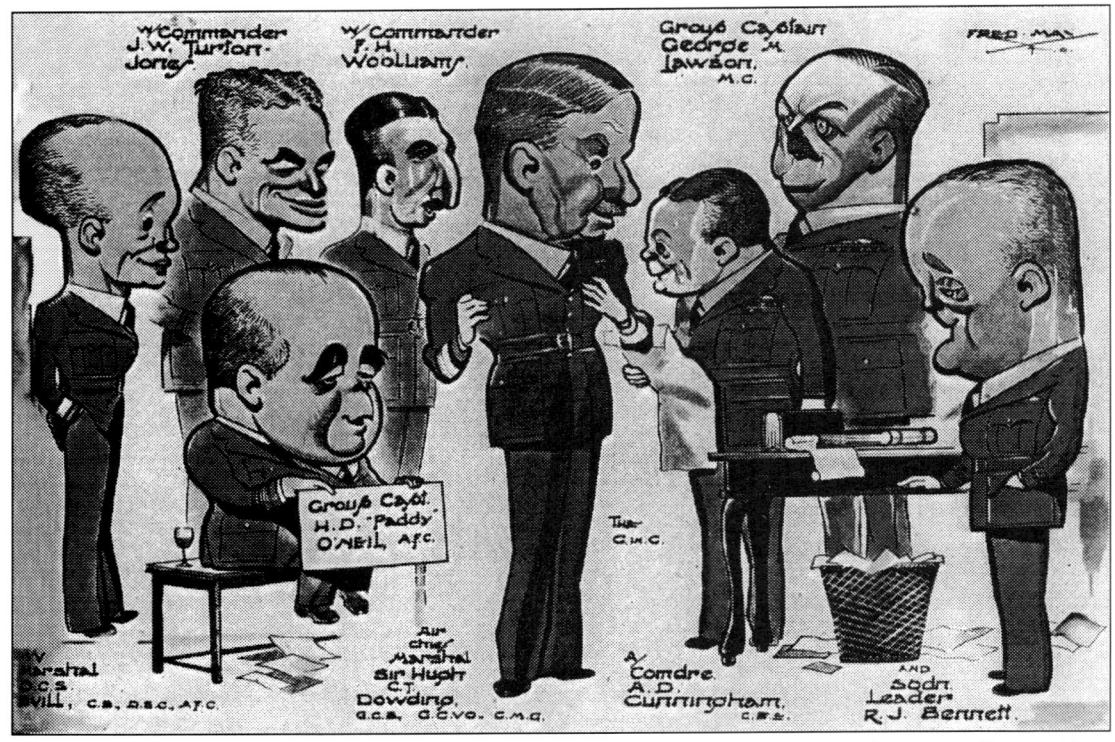

Major Fred May was Ground Liason Officer at HQ Fighter Command - he was also an artist and cartoonist. Here are his of some his representations of the Fighter Command Staff in 1940. [via Phillip May]

The new operations block

By far the most significant event during the spring of 1940 was the opening of the new underground operations block on 9 March, some ten weeks behind schedule due to an altered specification and to the effects of several major landslides during the construction period. In less than three minutes, 167 operational telephone lines were switched from the redundant operations room and filter room to the new block, while the most vital lines of the Defence Teleprinter Network were switched instantly, others following suit later. A new PBX in the underground block came into use two days later, all 300 or more lines being switched within one minute. Apart from the Operations Room and Filter Room, the underground block housed offices for the AOC-in-C, the SASO, the Air Staff and the duty Intelligence Officer, a power house, filtration plant, a cypher room, coding apparatus, rest rooms and a cleaner's room. Over the site of the underground block camouflage netting disguised its existence. At ground level, more new buildings, including quarters for unmarried sergeants, an office for the AA Battery staff, a gas clothing store, a rations store and a gas defence centre, were rapidly coming into use.

Ironically, the SASO, AVM Keith Park, was taken ill with appendicitis on the day before the new Operations Block came into use, and his position was filled temporarily by Gp. Capt. A. H. Orlebar until Air Cdre. A. D. Cunningham CBE was able to take over. Park did not return to Bentley Priory, instead moving to take over as AOC of 11 Group at Uxbridge when he recovered.

Controllers at Bentley Priory undertook three-hour watches. Their first duty in each watch was to study the log of the previous watch, followed by a view of the battle order of fighters and balloon barrages. Positions of convoys and fishing fleets were also noted. Reports of the

THE WAR YEARS

positions of the Home Fleet submarines, fighter patrols, private flights, civil airliners, RAF bombers, training exercises and searchlights all had to be studied so that orders could be issued to deal effectively with any given situation. Each controller was in constant touch with liaison officers, who provided all the information he required. He also gave permission for non-operational flights, setting their routes, times and signals to be used. He was certainly never idle!

The task carried out by the 'filterers' was a hectic one. Each person was in touch by dedicated telephone line with one RDF Station, which were situated on the coast looking outwards to sea. Readings taken from the radar plot at the RDF Station were converted there into grid references which were passed to the Filter Room to be marked by counters placed on an identical grid. As RDF Stations had overlapping areas of search they would record the same 'targets', enabling more accurate fixing of the positions of incoming raiders to be made. It was then possible for the track of the enemy aircraft to be determined and defensive action taken. After the intruder had passed over the English coast its continuing course was reported to the Operations Room by the Observer Corps, whose efforts were of the greatest possible value.

In the Operations Room at Bentley Priory and in similar rooms at Group and Sector level, information was received simultaneously via 'tellers' who were positioned on the balcony overlooking the plotting table in the Filter Room. Tellers followed the progress of aircraft movements in a designated area and 'told' the duty Controller and his staff the

Sir Fredrick Pile, C-in-C AA Command

'The Warren', a house opposite St. Peter's church at Bushey Heath, was taken over in September 1939 as a hostel for members of the WAAF. [J. Clarke]

ROYAL AIR FORCE
CONTROL AND REPORTING SYSTEM
during the Battle of Britain 1940

Key

<<<<<<<< Filtered information from RDF Stations
••••••••••• Unfiltered information from RDF Stations
- - - - - - - Observer Corps information
-o-o-o-o-o- Information from other sources
+++++++++ Combined information

John Jamlin 1997

THE WAR YEARS

In spite of a coating of green camouflage paint, Bentley Priory remained highly identifiable. [AVM 'Sandy' Johnstone]

position of each raid. Keeping a watchful eye on proceedings were Naval liaison officers whose job it was to take appropriate action should a raid on Naval facilities develop. Also taking a very active part in the proceedings was the Air Raid Warning section, tasked with controlling 130 Warning Districts responsible for alerting the civilian population.

One of the tellers in the underground block was ACW Trouncer, who recalls being on duty with Sgt. Yeo-Thomas, who in later years found fame working with the French Resistance as the 'White Rabbit'. His family had lived in France since the 1850s, and he had been business manager of Molyneux before the war. 'Tommy' took Elizabeth Trouncer out to dinner on a couple of occasions, but it transpired that this was merely so that he could be given a proper introduction to another WAAF, Barbara, with whom he had fallen in love and who he later married!

Raids on Great Britain became bigger, and the tellers found that the sight of plaques marking the approach of 300 or more bombers could be unnerving. ACW Trouncer was working on the French desk one day early in 1940 when she took a telephone call from Armentières, the message being that the Germans had arrived in the town and that the operations room there was being destroyed and the occupants evacuated, and ACM Dowding was to be informed. *"I got up and went and told him"*, she recalls, *"and he said 'Thank you; go back to your desk and get on with your work'. That was the last time I ever spoke to the great man"*.

Outside their strenuous working hours, airmen and WAAFs alike took part in social and sporting activities which included visiting the local hostelries, dancing, tennis, hockey and swimming. Sadly, tragedy struck on 25 April 1940, when a young airman, 746364 AC1 Neal,

RAF BENTLEY PRIORY AND STANMORE PARK

drowned while swimming at Watford baths. He was buried at Bushey on 30 April with full military honours. Close to the Priory was a pub much frequented by RAF personnel. A Warrant Officer and a Sergeant were found to have been selling sausages to the publican, who resold them to a hungry public!

Movements of army personnel during the spring of 1940 involved the departure of the 32nd Bn. LAA, which was replaced by a detachment of the 97th AA Bn., and the arrival of the 275th Bn. Honourable Artillery Company, which took over from the 285th Bn. The 275th Bn. moved out on 18 May and were replaced by the 32nd. LAA Bn., to whom were added 60 men of the QV Rifles for ground defence duties under their CO, Maj. Samuelson. They stayed only until 12 June, when a detachment of Scots Guards under Capt. J. A. Duncan MP took over.

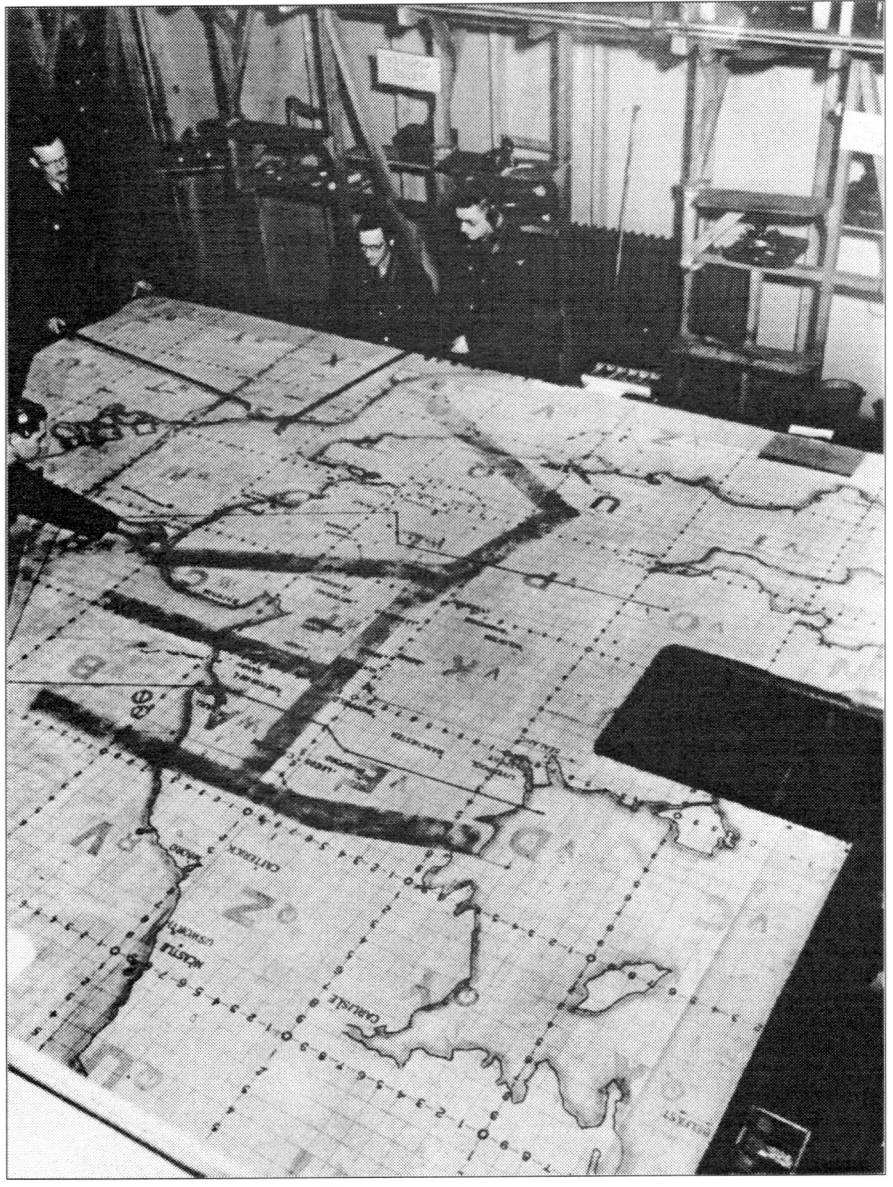

On this picture of the temporary Operations Room plotting table the large map of most of the UK can be seen, clearly marked with a grid. The picture makes much more sense when rotated to be viewed 'upside down'!

The larger squares are 100 x 100 kilometres, each of which is broken down into 100 10km. squares. Major towns and airfields are marked on the map, probably in different colours. Group boundaries are shown in thin soldi lines, although the meaning of the broad bands is unknown. [Crown copyright]

THE WAR YEARS

Two army officers manning the AA Defence position in the Bentley Priory Operations Room early in 1940. With the information they obtained from the plotting table below, they warned AA batteries about impending raids. The highly temporary nature given the circumstances is clearly evident, with paper notices pinned to bare board and wires and cables everywhere. [Crown copyright]

German troops advance in Europe

Unknown of course even to those who would take part, the campaign we know as the Battle of Britain, in which RAF Bentley Priory would play an inestimable part, was about to commence. Its root cause was the German invasion of Belgium and Holland on 10 May 1940 and entry into France three days later. British troops began their retreat from France on 26 May, most leaving by 4 June, but many only escaping by way of Dunkirk on 17 June. The last RAF squadrons of the AASF flew out on 18 June, and within hours a hundred Luftwaffe bombers made a heavy raid on targets in south-east England, the first in a concerted campaign covering several parts of the country. On 22 June France and Germany signed a peace pact, and Great Britain stood alone.

With the distinct possibility of invasion in mind, the Air Ministry decided that all airmen must attend a course in ground defence in order to be able to support the army personnel whose main task it was. Exercises were held in infiltration from outside the Station, which was successfully defended. Before long, Defence Squadrons, trained by army NCOs, came into being, and the squadron at Bentley Priory was formed in April 1940 under the command of Flg. Off. Seymour.

In the face of the tremendous threat to our country, flexibility of fighter squadrons had to be maintained, and it was for this main reason that removal of VHF radios installed in eight squadrons was ordered on 18 May. However, re-installation of these sets into seven squadrons of Blenheims, together with the provision of AI (Airborne Interception) radar, was authorised three weeks later. The quantity of mobile radio equipment for use in Fighter Command had also been increased, so that by June three mobile W/T stations, 44 R/T tenders (vehicles) and 150 portable sets were ready for use. Another scheme set up in June with Bentley Priory as its control station was known as 'Beetle'. An emergency inter-Service signals organisation, 'Beetle's' task was the rapid transmission by W/T of up-to-the-moment information on possible, or even probable, enemy assaults by parachutists or landings by sea or by aircraft. Such coded messages were sent to HQ Home Forces, to the three RAF operational Commands and five Army HQs and to the Navy and were then re-broadcast by R/T to lower-grade units. Coincidental with the 'Beetle' operations, the RAF Despatch Rider Letter Service was set up on 25 June at Bentley

RAF BENTLEY PRIORY AND STANMORE PARK

The Naval liaison officer at Fighter Command HQ, Bentley Priory, in 1940. A piece of brown paper shielding the table lamp sums up the contemporary 'make-do-and-mend' policy! From the calender on the officer's desk, just underneath the lamp it is possible to make out that the first thirteen days of September have been 'crossed through' indicating that this and the other pictures in the series may well have been taken on 14 September 1940, just one day before the Battle of Britain reached its climax! [Crown copyright]

Priory, the riders operating a number of scheduled routes in order to deliver written messages as quickly as possible.

Fitting of VHF radio sets to fighter aircraft soon presented problems. On 1 June ACM Dowding sent a message to Air Ministry — *"Owing to inadequate supplies it is necessary to suspend indefinitely the use of VHF by fighters, which will result in a reduction in efficiency"*. On the same day Dowding notified 11, 12 and 13 Groups *"I observe that accidents due to gross carelessness continue to occur in spite of the preciousness [sic] of every fighter aircraft. I wish you to impose dramatic and humiliating punishment in all such cases"*. The high spirits of the average fighter pilot were thus dampened down by the stern Dowding, an action he had to take before the situation became intolerable.

As a means of thanking Fighter Command personnel for their part in the recent evacuation from France, the Secretary of State for Air wrote to Dowding on 5 June 1940 via Sir Archibald Sinclair.

THE WAR YEARS

At least eight WAAF plotters can be seen in this view of the Filter Room in the Priory in early 1940. Scaffolding poles and timbers hold up the balcony! [Crown copyright]

He asked Dowding to convey to all ranks in his Command the following message — *"The War Cabinet has expressed their high appreciation of the fine work of the RAF in covering the evacuation of the British and French forces from Dunkirk. All ranks have done magnificently"*.

Two new outstations, code-named 'Radium' and 'Magic', had by now been set up for emergency use. 'Radium', to where seventeen airmen were posted from Bentley Priory in early June 1940, was at Radlett.

Investigations into suspected enemy radio-navigation aids were instigated by the Deputy Director of Signals at the Air Ministry in June 1940, for which task a number of personnel were posted to Bentley Priory. Listening stations were established at several RDF sites, from where the operators reported to a control centre set up in the operations block at Bentley Priory, code-named 'Headache'. Aircraft used by the Beam Approach Development Unit at Boscombe Down and equipped with special radio receivers were put at the disposal of the 'Headache' controller, and 54 flights were made. Following this, a new section of the Air Ministry, to be known as Radio Counter Measures, was set up.

Completing a stint of defending Bentley Priory, the 32nd. and 97th. Bns. RA moved out on 29 June and were replaced by the 33rd. and 145th. LAA Batteries, although the 33rd. stayed only a few days before giving way on 11 July to the 3rd. LAA Battery. With the possibility of an imminent invasion, sixty men of the Irish Guards arrived on 1 September for defence duty, but they left on 27 September, to be replaced by a detachment of the 50th. Bn. Royal Fusiliers.

A new unit, formed at Bentley Priory on 10 June 1940, was the Controllers' Training Unit (CTU), set up to train would-be fighter controllers. The intention was that the old Operations Room should be used for this purpose, but due to a number of problems a redundant room at

RAF BENTLEY PRIORY AND STANMORE PARK

An Army Anti-Aircraft gun crew takes a break for a 'char and a wad' during the Battle of Britain.

RAF Northolt was taken over by the CTU and the nucleus of staff moved there on 15 June.

The Battle of Britain

Although the Battle of Britain did not begin officially until 8 August 1940, the Luftwaffe had inflicted large-scale night raids on wide-ranging targets from 18 June, and daylight raids had begun on 1 July, when Hull was attacked. Germany's intention was to achieve air superiority before launching an invasion, which would mean the subjugation of the British people and effectively total victory in Europe. At Bentley Priory, the system was now working well, and Fighter Command was ready and waiting. The Order of Battle for 10 July shows 29 squadrons of Hurricanes, 19 of Spitfires, seven of twin-engined Blenheims and two of Defiant night-fighters, a total of 57 squadrons, to defend these islands against an onslaught which might well be devastating. Hitler's directive dated 16 July stated clearly that in view of the fact that Great Britain showed no inclination to "come to an understanding" he had decided to prepare an invasion of England. This was an ultimatum to be taken seriously, because ranged against the RAF were 1200 long-range bombers, 280 dive-bombers (Stukas), 760 single-engined fighters, 220 twin-engined fighters and 140 reconnaissance aircraft of the Luftwaffe. Although not all of these would be serviceable at any one time, they presented a major threat.

The day-to-day picture of the Battle of Britain has been well-documented in many books already, and needs no repetition here. Suffice it to say that the staff of Fighter Command's Operations Room and other sections were stretched to the limit, but, like Great Britain itself, they won through against all odds. Morale at Bentley Priory was boosted by the visits of several very important people, including HRH the Duke of Kent on 5 July and Their

Aircraft losses on both sides during The Battle of Britain

The losses on both sides during the battle are still open to discussion, as is the period over which it took place. What follows below are the aircraft that were recorded as being of total loss, missing or destroyed - it does not include those which suffered major damage but could eventually be repaired - over the months of July to October 1940 inclusive. The figures are divided into combat and non-combat categories.

Losses	RAF		Luftwaffe	
Date	C	N/C	C	N/C
1/7	1	-	10	1
2/7	-	-	3	1
3/7	-	1	4	1
4/7	1	2	3	2
5/7	1	3	2	1
6/7	-	2	3	2
7/7	6	-	5	1
8/7	4	-	7	2
9/7	6	-	11	2
10/7	1	-	8	1
11/7	6	1	15	2
12/7	3	5	8	-
13/7	3	2	6	-
14/7	-	-	3	-
15/7	1	2	4	-
16/7	-	-	2	1
17/7	1	-	2	2
18/7	5	1	5	1
19/7	10	-	4	1
20/7	6	2	14	1
21/7	1	1	7	3
22/7	-	2	2	-
22/7	-	4	3	3
24/7	2	2	10	2
25/7	6	1	16	-
26/7	2	2	2	-
27/7	1	2	4	-
28/7	4	1	9	1
29/7	3	1	12	-
30/7	-	1	4	3
31/7	2	3	2	1
Total	76	41	190	35

Date	C	N/C	C	N/C
1/8	1	1	12	4
2/8	-	2	3	2
3/8	-	-	3	1
4/8	-	2	1	5
5/8	2	-	1	2
6/8	-	5	1	2
7/8	-	5	4	1
8/8	15	2	21	1
9/8	-	2	3	1
10/8	-	-	-	1
11/8	30	2	35	1
12/8	20	1	27	-
13/8	13	1	34	1
14/8	4	3	19	2
15/8	28	17	71	-
16/8	22	6	44	2
17/8	-	2	1	-
18/8	35	8	60	-
19/8	4	1	4	4
20/8	2	-	6	2
21/8	1	3	13	-
22/8	4	1	2	2
23/8	-	1	2	3
24/8	24	1	30	4
25/8	16	1	20	1
26/8	27	-	34	3
27/8	1	3	5	-
28/8	17	1	26	3
29/8	9	-	12	4
30/8	20	5	24	2
31/8	34	-	28	1
Total	329	76	546	55

Date	C	N/C	C	N/C
1/9	15	1	5	3
2/9	23	11	26	3
3/9	15	3	12	4
4/9	18	2	21	1
5/9	21	1	21	1
6/9	22	1	34	3
7/9	28	3	38	-
8/9	4	1	13	2
9/9	21	-	25	2
10/9	-	1	4	2
11/9	31	-	22	4
12/9	2	-	3	3
13/9	2	1	6	-
14/9	13	1	7	2
15/9	26	1	56	-
16/9	2	2	9	-
17/9	6	2	8	-
18/9	11	-	18	1
19/9	-	-	8	-
20/9	7	1	3	-
21/9	-	-	9	1
22/9	-	-	2	2
23/9	10	-	13	3
24/9	7	4	7	-
25/9	3	2	13	2
26/9	7	-	8	2
27/9	28	-	49	1
28/9	15	2	8	2
29/9	5	1	8	-
30/9	15	3	41	4
Total	357	44	497	48

Date	C	N/C	C	N/C
1/10	6	-	6	6
2/10	3	-	14	3
3/10	-	1	8	-
4/10	1	-	9	1
5/10	7	-	14	1
6/10	-	3	6	1
7/10	13	2	19	1
8/10	2	3	10	1
9/10	3	2	11	-
10/10	5	3	2	5
11/10	9	2	5	2
12/10	9	3	5	-
13/10	3	-	2	-
14/10	1	-	2	1
15/10	15	4	12	-
16/10	1	1	10	-
17/10	5	2	9	3
18/10	-	6	11	1
19/10	-	1	1	2
20/10	4	-	9	1
21/10	-	3	5	1
22/10	5	-	9	2
23/10	1	-	3	1
24/10	-	4	2	5
25/10	10	9	19	2
26/10	5	4	9	-
27/10	9	1	11	1
28/10	-	1	2	-
29/10	6	4	18	6
30/10	-	1	2	-
Total	123	60	245	47

Majesties the King and Queen on 6 September, a day on which scattered raids were taking place. In the Operations Room, they were able to watch a raid on London being plotted. On that same day, Maj. Gen. Strong, Brig. Gen. Delos C. Emmons and Maj. Studler of the US Army and Rear Admiral Gormley of the American Mission also visited, no doubt to see at first hand the techniques used so successfully by the RAF in fighter control. The Americans continued to show great interest, two Navy men, Capt. Kirk, the US Naval Attaché, and his assistant, Lt. Cdr. Hitchcock, arriving on 2 August, a relatively quiet day. Shortly afterwards, the US Ambassador was escorted to Bentley Priory by the Secretary of State for Air, Sir Archibald Sinclair. The Prime Minister came to monitor events on four occasions in August, once with Mrs. Churchill and once with Lord Beaverbrook, the Minister of Aircraft Production. During his visit on 4 August, Churchill asked Dowding to tell him how many fighters would suffice to defeat the enemy threat, and was told bluntly that eighty squadrons would do the trick.

Of increasing value to the overall defence of the country was the 'Y' Service,

Fighter Command Order of Battle*
15th September 1940

Squadron	Aircraft	Base	Sector
10 Group (HQ Rudloe Manor, near Bath)			
56	Hurricane	Boscombe Down	Middle Wallop.
87	Hurricane	Exeter & Bibury	Exeter.
601	Hurricane	Filton	Exeter.
23 (half)	Blenheim	Middle Wallop	Middle Wallop
238	Hurricane	Middle Wallop	Middle Wallop
604	Blenheim/Beaufighter	Middle Wallop	Middle Wallop
79	Hurricane	Pembrey	Filton.
247	Gladiator	Roborough	St Eval
234	Spitfire	St Eval	St Eval
236	Blenheim	St Eval	St Eval
152	Spitfire	Warmwell	Middle Wallop
609	Spitfire	Warmwell	Middle Wallop
11 Group (HQ Uxbridge, Middlesex)			
72	Spitfire	Biggin Hill	Biggin Hill
92	Spitfire	Biggin Hill	Biggin Hill
141 (half)	Defiant	Biggin Hill	Biggin Hill
605	Hurricane	Croydon	Kenley
17	Hurricane	Debden	Debden
73	Hurricane	Debden	Debden
23 (half)	Blenheim/Beaufighter	Ford	Tangmere
66	Spitfire	Gravesend	Biggin Hill
504	Hurricane	Hendon	Northolt
41	Spitfire	Hornchurch	Hornchurch
222	Spitfire	Hornchurch	Hornchurch
600	Blenheim/Beaufighter	Hornchurch	Hornchurch
603	Spitfire	Hornchurch	Hornchurch
253	Hurricane	Kenley	Kenley
501	Hurricane	Kenley	Kenley
25 (half)	Blenheim	Martlesham Heath	Debden
257	Hurricane	Martlesham Heath	Debden
1 (RCAF)	Hurricane	Northolt	Northolt
229	Hurricane	Northolt	Northolt
303	Hurricane	Northolt	Northolt

THE WAR YEARS

formed to collect and decipher information from enemy radio transmissions. The main interception centre manned by the RAF was at Cheadle in Cheshire, supplemented by a listening station at Kingsdown, Kent. There, R/T conversations from and to Luftwaffe pilots were collected from small listening stations around the south-east coast, manned by German-speaking WAAFs and WRNs. Information gleaned from the reports was fed to Sectors, Groups and Fighter Command, and eventually became so complete that the build-up of raids outside the range of RDF radar could be reported.

Data of all types were analysed by the Intelligence Section at Bentley Priory in order to build up as complete a picture of enemy activity as possible for the benefit of all who needed a daily report. Information came in from the Observer Corps posts, technical analyses of enemy aircraft shot down, reports filed by RAF pilots, in fact from any and every source of valid information.

Each day, unless he was visiting an operational Fighter Command airfield, ACM Dowding could be seen in the underground Operations complex — known to those who worked in it as 'The

25 (half)	Bleinheim/Beaufighter	North Weald	North Weald
249	Hurricane	North Weald	North Weald
46	Hurricane	Stapleford Tawney	North Weald
213	Hurricane	Tangmere	Tangmere
607	Hurricane	Tangmere	Tangmere
602	Spitfire	Westhampnett	Tangmere
12 Group (HQ Watnall, Nottinghamshire)			
85	Hurricane	Church Fenton	Church Fenton
306	Hurricane	Church Fenton	Church Fenton
29	Blenheim.Beaufighter	Digby	Digby
151	Hurricane	Digby	Digby
611	Spitfire	Digby	Digby
242	Hurricane	Duxford	Duxford
302	Hurricane	Duxford	Duxford
310	Hurricane	Duxford	Duxford
19	Spitfire	Fowlmere	Duxford
264	Defiant	Kirton-in-Lindsey	Kirton-in-Lindsey
616	Spitfire	Kirton-in-Lindsey	Kirton-in-Lindsey
64	Spitfire	Leconfield & Ringway	Church Fenton
1	Hurricane	Wittering	Wittering
74	Spitfire	Wittering	Coltishall
266	Spitfire	Wittering	Wittering
13 Group (HQ Ouston, Northumberland)			
32	Hurricane	Acklington	Usworth
219 (half)	Blenheim	Acklington	Usworth
601	Spitfire	Acklington	Usworth
245	Hurricane	Aldergrove	Aldergrove
54	Spitfire	Catterick	Catterick
219 (half)	Blenheim/Beaufighter	Catterick	Catterick
111	Hurricane	Drem	Turnhouse
263**	Hurricane/Whirlwind	Drem	Turnhouse
145	Hurricane	Dyce & Montrose	Dyce
232	Hurricane	Sumburgh	Wick
3	Hurricane	Turnhouse	Turnhouse
65	Spitfire	Turnhouse	Turnhouse
141	Defiant	Turnhouse	Turnhouse
43	Hurricane	Usworth	Usworth

* - excluding training and other non combat units.   ** - non-operational

'Hole' — keeping abreast of the current raid situation. The WAAFs who toiled on the plotting tables often hardly knew he was there, their attention being fully focussed on the task in hand, but when the pressure eased a little his murmured *"Well done"* was heard and appreciated. Staff at the Priory were encouraged to maintain a calm and dignified mien at all times, a quality which Dowding's personal assistant during the Battle of Britain, Robert Wright (later his biographer), saw as a *"...somewhat staid and old-fashioned family business office in a provincial town"*. By mid-August, Dowding could sense that the tide of battle was turning, and remarked to Gen. Pile of AA Command that *"England is being defended — saved — by four hundred young men"*.

Sunday 15 September 1940 was the day which is now generally regarded as being the decisive day in the Battle of Britain, and is the date which is now celebrated as Battle of Britain Day. Before beginning its efforts, the Luftwaffe paraded its vast fleet of bomber and fighter aircraft up and down the Channel in full view of British RDF radar, and at 11.00 the force turned towards the English coast. RAF fighters were of course waiting to repulse the enemy aircraft before they could reach their targets and succeeded in doing so, although a few bombers breached the defensive formations to hit London and Southampton. 56 Luftwaffe aircraft succumbed to air or ground defences at the expense of 27 RAF aircraft and fourteen pilots. Another attempt was made by the Luftwaffe in the afternoon, with no more success than before. The bombing was erratic, due largely to the enthusiasm with which the RAF fighter pilots, directed as usual by means of RDF from Group and Sector overseen by the staff of Bentley Priory's Operations Block, attacked the many formations of Luftwaffe bombers. By this time, Fighter Command had at its disposal 32 squadrons of Hurricanes, 19 of Spitfires, one full and three half-squadrons of Blenheims, three full squadrons and three half-squadrons of mixed Beaufighters and Blenheims, two full and two half-squadrons of Defiants and one squadron of venerable Gladiator biplanes, the equivalent of a total of 62 squadrons, still far short of Dowding's desired eighty.

Two days later, Hitler postponed Operation 'Sealion', his intended invasion of Great Britain, although he was still under the impression that an invasion was a practical proposition, even though the RAF had not been defeated, a factor hitherto considered to be vital. Instead, he decided to bomb civilian targets in retaliation for raids which the RAF had mounted on Berlin, a city which the German High Command had always claimed would never be attacked. London was the prime target from now on, and from that point the Fighter Command staff knew that Britain had not lost the war. Morale, Harold Gross recalls, was always high in the Operations Room. A great handicap to the RAF, however, was a total

Nationalities of those involved on the Allied side in the Battle of Britain.

	Number	Killed
Australian	22	14
Belgian	29	6
Canadian	94	20
Czech	87	8
Free French	14	0
Irish	10	0
Jamaican	1	0
New Zealand	101	14
Palestinian	1	0
Polish	147	30
South African	22	9
Southern Rhodesia	2	0
United Kingdom	2543	418
United States	7	1
Total	**3080**	**520**

THE WAR YEARS

A scene in the temporary Filter Room in the Priory, with a WAAF plotter laying a plaque containing raid information.
[Crown copyright]

lack of night fighters equipped with airborne radar, and the Luftwaffe took advantage of this fact by concentrating on night raids from the beginning of October.

On 17 September 80 (Signals) Wing was formed by the Air Ministry to take over the activities previously code-named 'Headache' in temporary premises at Radlett, thus relieving some congestion at Bentley Priory. From Radlett 80 Wing moved on 9 October to what had been the Aldenham Country Club at Elstree, part of Elstree airfield.

The final mass combat in the Battle of Britain took place on 30 September, when nearly twenty percent of the Luftwaffe raiders failed to return home, destroyed by RAF fighters and ground gunnery. On the same day, ACM Dowding was appointed as Knight Grand Commander of the Order of the Bath by HM King George VI.

Ground defence of the vital but vulnerable Bentley Priory during the Battle of Britain was undertaken by the local Defence Squadron, now under the command of Sqn. Ldr. Williamson.

Breathing space
Although the Battle of Britain was over, the war came perilously close to Bentley Priory on the night of 16 October 1940, when an RAF bomber crashed on the Station. Lost in bad weather, Wellington Mk.Ic N2771 of 311 (Polish) Sqn. was on its way back to base at East Wretham in Norfolk when severe icing caused it to lose height and come down on the sports field. Five of the six crew members died in the crash, and on 21 October were buried with full military honours at Pinner. Only the front gunner, badly burned, survived. Ironically, this British aircraft came closer to destroying the Priory complex than the Luftwaffe did! Enemy raids continued, and on 6 November three bombs hit the Station, one of them a direct hit on hut 71, but fortunately there were no casualties. Less lucky were the WAAFs who lived in

RAF BENTLEY PRIORY AND STANMORE PARK

Now a residential home for the elderly, 'Kestrel Grove' in Hive Road was designed in 1910 by Harold Goslett for Mr. W. B. Gair. It was requisitioned in 1943 to become the Headquarters Unit of the Allied Expeditionary Air Force and eventually the Headquarters of the Royal Observer Corps. [author]

'Rosary Priory' in Elstree Road, which received a direct hit on 15 November. The building was badly damaged, but there were no injuries to any of the WAAFs, who stayed very calm and helped the emergency services restore order.

The RDF system used so effectively during the recent Battle of Britain continued to be a focus of interest for the United States of America, which had not of course yet entered the war. Visiting Bentley Priory on 26 October 1940 to see the operating procedures were Maj. Edwards and Capt. Saville of the US Army, who were followed by Lt. Col. Taylor on 10 December. Another VIP visitor was Gen. Sikorski, Commander-in-Chief of Polish Forces, who was present on 10 October with four of his countrymen.

After five months at Northolt, the CTU moved into requisitioned premises, 'Woodlands', in Clamp Hill, Stanmore, on 8 November 1940. Six days later the Radio-Telephone Speech Unit arrived from Uxbridge and was absorbed into CTU. Subjects covered during the three-week course included navigation, RDF, the organisation of AA Command, searchlights, night flying, signals, R/T procedure, maps, convoys, fighter tactics, meteorology, instruments, codes and cyphers, fighter tactics, ground-controlled and airborne interception. One wonders what the students did in their spare time! Among them were members of the Fleet Air Arm and a number of Polish officers.

Improvements to the defences
Meanwhile, measures to improve the system further continued apace. On 23 November a VHF radio link with Air Ministry in Whitehall was established, using Eddistone Type 215A transmitter/receivers working on 78.0/78.5 MHz, with a connection to the telephone exchange at each end. The fitting of Fighter Command aircraft with VHF radio also continued, so that by the end of November 35 squadrons had been equipped. Beaufighter night-fighters were being fitted with either AI Mk.IV or a

THE WAR YEARS

version of the Lorenz system (a German invention!). Fifteen sector stations had also been provided with temporary mobile VHF sets. In December, progress was accelerated so that all squadrons would be using VHF by March 1941.

A radical move towards the effective campaign against enemy bombers, particularly at night, came into trial use at Durrington in Sussex late in October 1940. Known as Ground Controlled Interception (GCI), the new equipment enabled a controller watching blips on a radar screen to direct his fighter force by R/T to a position from which an attack could be made, often with the added help of the fighter's own AI radar. This was a major step forward, relieving controllers at the various Operations Rooms of a good deal of the pressure.

The task of the plotters at Bentley Priory is recalled with great nostalgia by Mrs. Anthea Shepherd. Aged eighteen and with School Certificate and Matriculation to her credit, Anthea had enrolled in October 1940 at Adastral House, Kingsway and as 425199 ACW2 Hammick A. had been given two weeks basic training at Harrogate, Yorkshire. She was then selected for trade training as a plotter (Clerk/SD) at Leighton Buzzard. This training period was also two weeks, during which time she was billeted in an old workhouse, and remembers that to reach the ablutions an external walkway had to be used, a most unpleasant journey in the November weather! Training completed, Anthea, now an ACW1, reported to RAF Bentley Priory just at a time of major effort, and wondered what she had let herself in for!

Plotters were divided into three shifts of about thirty personnel each — two of them comprising WAAFs and one of RAF

In the underground Operations Room which came into use in March 1940 there was a little more space. The electrically-operated 'cues' of which details are given in the text are seen in use in this picture. [Crown copyright]

RAF BENTLEY PRIORY AND STANMORE PARK

'Woodlands' in Clamp Hill was used by the Controllers' Training Unit from November 1940. After the war it became offices for the local authority and eventually fell into decay before being demolished. This picture was taken in happier days in the 1930s. [Harrow local history collection]

men ('C' Watch), as it was considered by certain senior officers that it would be wrong for the two genders to have physical contact during working hours! One shift worked from midnight to 0800; another from 08.00 to 12.00 and from 16.00 to 20.00; and the third shift from 12.00 to 16.00 and from 20.00 to midnight. Plotters changed their shifts every two weeks. On duty, they took details of incoming raids through headphones from the Filter Room staff, who had received raw information from the RDF Stations and Observer Corps. Plotters at Fighter Command HQ used not a croupier's type of rake, as is often imagined, but a metal rod four or five feet long down which an electrical charge was sent from a modified torch to magnetize a shaped end-piece. As long as the torch switch remained pressed, an arrow-shaped piece of tin about 3/4" (20mm.) long could be picked up and deposited in an appropriate position on the plotting table. Arrows were coloured red, blue or yellow to correspond with a clock, visible to all plotters, on the face of which each five-minute interval was coloured differently, the plotters at Bentley Priory being involved only with the final fifteen minutes of the approach of a raid. Grid lines were painted on the table at 12" (30cm.) intervals in each direction, each resulting square carrying a reference number. Each raid was allocated a number, and the extent of the raid was 'told' to two people manning a blackboard which was readily visible to all concerned. On the balcony above, officers could see the complete picture and notify sector and Group operations rooms accordingly. Liaison officers from AA Command, the ARP section, the Royal Navy and the Met. Office were also in a good position to make use of the up-to-date information thus displayed. During their shift, the plotters worked for forty-minute periods, with short breaks in between.

In addition to the plotters, there was a WAAF 'tracer' who sat on the balcony overlooking the plotting table and whose task was to draw on large sheets of paper, printed with a matching grid, the track of

THE WAR YEARS

His Majesty King George VI, on a visit to RAF Bentley Priory, walks with a typically serious ACM Sir Hugh Dowding. Like most people, both are carrying gas-masks in case of a gas attack. ['Chic' Willett]

the raids and their quantified extent, for analysis by the Intelligence staff and for record purposes.

ACW1 Hammick lived with other plotters in one of a group of requisitioned houses near the north end of Marsh Lane, Stanmore. Half an hour or so before the start of their shift they were collected by bus, which took them almost to the end of the ramp leading down into the underground operations block, so they were hardly aware of the rest of the complex and certainly never entered the Priory building. During their break periods or at times of aerial inactivity the girls often curled up on Lloyd Loom chairs in their rest room (where males were forbidden to enter!). In a tiny kitchen they made tea, or in the absence of anything else, Camp coffee. Much off-watch time was spent in cheerful 'gossip', but the general atmosphere was one of dedication to the task when needed. Theirs was a classless society, and everyone 'mucked in'.

The stamina of youth is demonstrated by a sudden decision made by four of the plotters, including Anthea Hammick, when coming off duty at 08.00 one summer morning. Being such a glorious day, they decided that they would rather spend it in the open air than in bed. Without any further ado, they hitch-hiked in high spirits to Marlow, where they hired a punt with the idea of drifting down the River Thames and having a few hours' sleep in a quiet place. Things did not go according to plan, however, and they had to return sleepless to Stanmore to ready themselves for their next period of duty. The 'tube' line at Stanmore being so close, the WAAF girls travelled into the West End to visit a cinema or go shopping as often as finances allowed.

Departure of Dowding

Air Chief Marshal Dowding, now aged 58 and with four years of ever-increasing stress behind him, was by now overdue for retirement, which had been deferred several times already, although he felt that he should carry on until the spring of 1942. However, Dowding did not have the confidence of two retired officers, Marshals of the Royal Air Force Sir John Salmond and Sir Hugh Trenchard, who considered that Dowding had failed in his task of defending Great Britain against night raids. They applied pressure on Lord Beaverbrook and on the Prime Minister, Winston Churchill, who had the utmost faith in Dowding, to remove him from office. On 13 November 1940 Dowding met the Secretary of State for Air, Sir Archibald Sinclair, who told him that Lord Beaverbrook, who was deeply involved in the procurement of aircraft in the United States, had asked for Dowding's assistance in that task, and added that a replacement as AOC-in-C Fighter Command had already been arranged. After visiting the first GCI Station at Durrington, Dowding wrote his final report on the subject of night-time interception on 17 November, and one week later left Bentley Priory, a victim of political intrigue. He was

RAF BENTLEY PRIORY AND STANMORE PARK

"My dear Fighters boys..."
It was not only the day fighters that won the Battle of Britain controlled from Bentley Priory, but the night-fighters also. Left is K7157 (YX:N) a Bristol Blenheim IF Night Fighter from 54 OTU whilst below relaxing as far as possible during stand-by between sorties are aircrew from 600 Sqn.

succeeded as AOC-in-C on 25 November by Air Marshal Sir W. Sholto Douglas KCB MC DFC, but before departing he sent a message to all Fighter Command Stations and squadrons:

"My dear Fighter Boys,
In sending you this my last message, I wish I could say all that is in my heart. I cannot hope to surpass the simple eloquence of the Prime minister's words, 'Never before has so much been owed by so many to so few'. The debt remains and will increase.

In saying goodbye to you I want you to know how continually you have been in my thoughts, and that, though our direct connection may be severed, I may yet be able to help you in your gallant fight.
Goodbye to you and God bless you all"

Dowding's foresight in refusing to send more fighter squadrons to France before that country fell provided the resources and the time to rebuild which turned out to be vital in winning the Battle of Britain. It is therefore very surprising that the official 1941 history of the Battle of Britain does

THE WAR YEARS

Other night fighter types used by the RAF included Bristol Beaufighters like T4638 NG:F of 604 Squadron {R. Sturtivant].

not even mention him, and unlike his successor he never received further promotion. Gen. Sir Frederick Pile, C-in-C of AA Command, later said of Dowding *"Of the great service leaders, Dowding was the outstanding airman I met in the war. A difficult man, self-opinionated, and a man who knew more than anybody about all aspects of aerial warfare... ...history will undoubtedly record his contribution to the Allied victory".*

With the tension relaxed a little, time was found for more sport and social activity. In November 1940, six cinema shows and six dances were held, while out on the sports field (which had been requisitioned from the Colne Valley Water Co.) three Rugby football and six soccer matches were played. Just before Christmas a party for children of service and civilian personnel was much enjoyed, not least by the adults running it!

Defence after dark

The new AOC-in-C made night air defence a priority and quickly brought together a number of officers to staff a new branch at Fighter Command HQ, to be known as Ops.3. This branch was put under the command of Air Cdre. A. H. Orlebar, who as a Sqn. Ldr. had achieved fame in 1929 when commanding the High Speed Flight by setting a world record speed of 357.7 mph (approx. 575 kph) in a Supermarine S.6 floatplane on 12 September 1929, just a few days after the British triumph in the Schneider Trophy race. In overall charge of the three Operations branches (Ops.1 handling daytime air defence and Ops.2 Control & Reporting) was the SASO, AVM W. B. Callaway CBE AFC. A task of prime importance was to establish an Operational Training Unit for night-fighter crews, and this was opened at Church Fenton in Yorkshire as 54 OTU on 25 November 1940. There, qualified AI radar operators were now brought together with pilots to fly Blenheim, Havoc and Defiant night-fighters pending the availability of AI-equipped Beaufighters. It was some time, however, before the expanding night fighter units of the RAF began to have a significant effect on the Luftwaffe raiders. A member of Ops.3, the late Air Cdre. H. M. Pearson CBE, records in his autobiography that Air Cdre. Orlebar worked so incessantly on the task of combating night-time raids that he almost suffered a breakdown in health. To prevent this happening, one of his colleagues took Orlebar's office keys home each evening, with his consent, thus enforcing some relaxation on this dedicated officer. In the Intelligence section at Fighter Command HQ, Wg. Cdr. W. E. Coope was appointed head on 9 December in place of Wg. Cdr. Lord G. N. Douglas-Hamilton.

Visiting the WAAFs on 12 December

RAF BENTLEY PRIORY AND STANMORE PARK

1940 was HRH the Duchess of Gloucester. Unfortunately, an accident involving a service coach caused the death two days later of one of the WAAFs, 889772 ACW1 Pullen J, who was buried at Northwood on 19 December with full military honours.

The 3rd LAA Battery left Bentley Priory on 1 December and was replaced by the 33rd., which stayed two weeks before moving on, its successor being the 32nd. LAA Battery. At the end of December 1940, RAF Bentley Priory was staffed by 667 RAF personnel, 380 WAAFs and 379 soldiers. Those of Scottish origin, and doubtless many others, joined in a Hogmanay ceremony arranged by the officers and men of the Scots Guards on 1 January 1941.

Gp. Capt. HRH the Duke of Kent reported for duty as Fighter Command Welfare Officer at Bentley Priory on 6 January, a position he held when he lost his life in the crash of a Sunderland flying-boat near Oban in Scotland on 25 August 1942. He would probably have been active after the raid on 30 January, when a number of incendiary bombs fell in the grounds of *'Glenthorn'* and more in Sir Harold Bellman's property in Priory Close, adjacent to Bentley Priory.

Many visits of interested parties took place during January 1941, significant visitors being AVM Breadner, the CAS of the RCAF; Col. Taylor from the US Embassy; the Lord Mayor of London; pioneer aviator Mr. Tom Sopwith; MRAF Sir John Salmond; and the Secretary of State for Air, Sir Archibald Sinclair. During the month it was proposed by the Air Ministry that the Director of Rescue Services should be stationed at Bentley Priory, where rapid communications facilities were available. So far, no dedicated search and rescue organisation existed for the benefit of aircrews who had ditched in the Channel, although fifteen boats were coming into service with the Royal Navy.

In February 1941 much movement of army personnel took place. The 32nd LAA Batt. left on 8 February and were replaced by the 208th LAA Batt., and ten days later 120 more Scots Guards took over from the detachment of Grenadiers. At the end of the month 799 RAF men, 518 WAAFs and 588 soldiers made up the 1905 personnel attached to Bentley Priory. War Weapons Week at Bushey included a parade on 29 March in which RAF, WAAF and Scots Guards took part, headed by pipers and drummers, and this event was repeated at Radlett on 27 April.

Photographs taken by a Coastal Command aircraft early in March 1941 showed that the camouflage of the Bentley Priory buildings was inadequate, although it was recognised that camouflage of the many new flat-roofed buildings was almost impossible. Since the German authorities knew before the war of the existence of the Fighter Command headquarters, it was reasoned that they might now believe that the headquarters had moved, and it was therefore suggested that the buildings should be made to appear derelict!

It was stated in March 1941 by the AOC-in-C that in his view 1941 would be critical in defending the country from the German onslaught. Once we had successfully repulsed the enemy we could switch our efforts onto the offensive, he believed. More fighter squadrons would therefore be needed in 1941 than in the following year — 80 day and 20 night squadrons, an increase of eight day fighter squadrons. The SASO considered, in the light of experience during the Battle of Britain, that he should be kept better informed on events, and asked for an officer of Sqn. Ldr. rank to become his personal assistant. Before long, it was decided that information on operations should be made readily available to those members of the Air Staff not working in the underground operations block, and an office eventually known as the Fighter Command War Room was opened under the control of Gp. Capt. Lawson.

The first UFOs?
Mystifying echoes began appearing on RDF Station radar screens in March 1941, consisting of a large number of echoes at long range, sometimes showing movement

THE WAR YEARS

towards the English coast at 20 to 40 miles per hour (32 to 64 kph). At times the echoes would remain visible for several hours before fading away, and were often seen when heavy enemy air raids were in progress. There were also single echoes which appeared to hover more or less stationary. A Beaufighter aircraft sent to investigate one of these found that the 'target' took evasive action but returned after the Beaufighter had left! The AOC-in-C demanded action to find out the cause of the echoes, perhaps by a Whitley aircraft of 80 Group, but there the matter seems to have rested.

Movement 'Macaroon' was a mock alert to test the rapid deployment of staff to the emergency operations complex. On 31 March at 10.55 an alert was received and all personnel were notified within twenty minutes and instructed to assemble at 14.45 for a 15.00 departure. Officers left Bentley Priory in three cars, other ranks by coach, which travelled to Leighton Buzzard, where they reported in at the Poor Law Institute before moving on to the emergency operations room. Officers spent the night at Potsgrove Rectory, other ranks at the Poor Law Institute. At 08.30 next morning the exercise was cancelled and everyone returned to Bentley Priory, presumably having gained some valuable experience.

By April 1941, VHF radio had been installed in all squadrons and operational elements of Fighter Command. The Operational Training Units (OTU) which trained new fighter pilots were not being equipped, apart from 54 OTU at Church Fenton, due to a lack of available frequencies, which would not be available until the spring of 1942, when TR.1143 radio sets would come into use. The first transportable GCI equipment had given a great deal of trouble, as the aerials were weak and tuning gear did not function properly. Its range was limited to 4 miles (6.4km.). By the end of April eleven GCI Stations were operational.

During April 1941 the AOC-in-C expressed concern about the comparative performance of RAF and Luftwaffe aircraft. He stressed that the new Typhoon fighter-bomber should be put into production as quickly as possible, venturing to suggest that if the RAF did not receive some by the end of the summer they could be too late, as the war in the air might already have been lost! He did not agree with Air Marshal Joubert de la Ferté, who had proposed to reduce the strength of the Observer Corps as GCI became more efficient, retorting that GCI could not read plots below an altitude of 7000 feet (2135m.). Furthermore, in May Sholto Douglas remarked that one method of reducing staff numbers would be to reduce those working in the Intelligence Section!

Members of the Observer Corps at Bentley Priory and at the many Centres and Posts were delighted in April 1941 to hear that His Majesty the King had consented to the addition of the word Royal to the Corps' title in recognition of the outstanding work carried out since before the outbreak of war. Soon afterwards, authority for the first female members of the Corps was given, and by the end of the war many had joined, adding to the efficiency of the ROC.

The Intelligence Section at Bentley Priory had, by May 1941, completed studies of Luftwaffe airfields in occupied territory, German night navigation methods, night fighter tactics and radio control of enemy day fighters. In June an organisation was proposed for the correlation of the tracks of enemy aircraft, which normally were only referred to when investigation of a specific raid was required. Thus the activities of the enemy were not under continuous review. It was believed that a more accurate picture could be produced, although this task would take up to five days.

Living conditions at and around Bentley Priory continued to improve, and the opening on 9 June of a new canteen for the WAAF and female civilian employees in the old Central Registry was a major step forward. Mrs. Barbara Darnell, then ACW Thatcher, was billeted at 'The Warren' in Bushey High Road, and recalls

RAF BENTLEY PRIORY AND STANMORE PARK

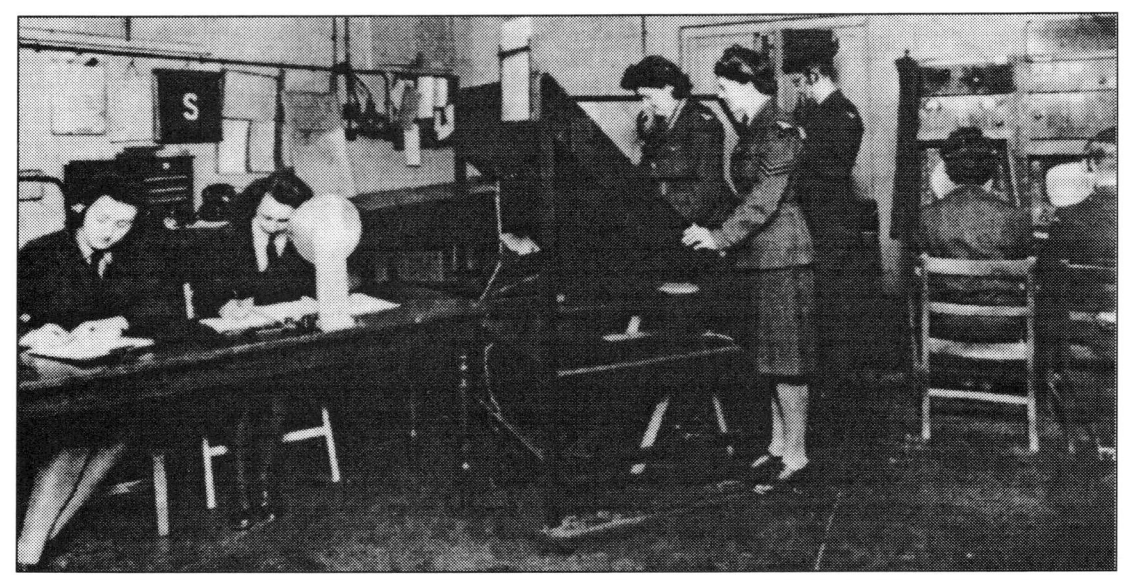

The Receiver Room at a Chain Home Radar Station. These receiving centres were linked by land-line to Bentley Priory.

being in the bath when a bomb fell nearby, blowing in the bathroom door, which took her by surprise and created a nasty draught! Her room-mate at one stage was a titled lady [whose name was supplied to the author but withheld!] who had no idea what to do with her clothes, so dropped them onto the floor after use. Before joining the WAAF her clothing had been whisked away, to reappear later clean and folded and put away tidily. Her dilemma was sad to behold when she shoved them into a drawer and hoped for the best! A lesson in the use of a laundry bundle, tied with string and labelled, was duly given. During exceptionally hot weather some of the girls, after night duty, slept in the nearby orchard without benefit of night-clothes, and after certain fighter pilots somehow became aware of this fact the girls' sleep was much disturbed by low-flying aircraft!

During the 'blitz' of 1941/42, the plotters in the 'Hole' worked watches of four hours on duty and four hours off, although the off-duty periods were diminished by the long climb to the surface, the time taken for the coach to take the girls to their hostels for a meal and a bath before they flopped into bed for a pitifully short sleep. The process was then reversed (apart from the bath) and the plotters took over the watch and plugged into their allotted CH RDF Stations. ACW Thatcher remembers chatting to whoever was at the other end of the line until a blip appeared on their radar screen and a plot was given. She then placed a small coloured arrow on the appropriate grid reference on the filter table, and the situation was duly dealt with by the filter Officer. When she had become a competent plotter, ACW Thatcher was allocated to the CH Station regarded as the crème-de-la-crème, Dunkirk in Kent, near the narrowest part of the English Channel. Plots came through thick and fast at times, the table became saturated and the brain followed suit, but somehow the plotters survived.

Another of the WAAFs in the Bentley Priory Operations Room had been the fiancée of fighter ace 'Cobber' Cain, a New Zealander who had won the DFC in France in the early days of the war but had been killed while performing aerobatics in a Spitfire. She was, apparently, a blonde who liked a good time, a budding actress, always full of good humour, though possibly covering her feelings at the death of her fiancée. Her friendship with ACW Thatcher was considered surprising, as

THE WAR YEARS

there was great rivalry between the Ops. Room plotters and those in the Filter Room, who thought the Ops. Room girls had a 'cushy' job compared with theirs! 'Cobber's' sister was also involved in plotting, as she was an operator at one of the CH Stations.

American involvement

Early covert United States activity in the United Kingdom is revealed in a memo, top secret at the time, from Sholto Douglas to the Air Ministry on 10 June 1941 under reference WSD/43. In it he wrote *"If the US fighter squadrons are to operate within the Fighter Command system, it is essential that they should be equipped with VHF R/T. Without it, their power to protect American bases will be seriously compromised. It is suggested that the US authorities should be approached at once with a view to having the aircraft with which the ten squadrons earmarked for the defence of the US bases in Northern Ireland and western Scotland are equipped modified to take VHF"*. This was six months before Japan attacked Pearl Harbour and Hitler declared war on the United States! There were no American bases and no American fighter squadrons in this country - the United States was neutral, and President Frederick Delano Roosevelt was under considerable pressure from pro-German and other sources within his country to keep it so. In a further letter under the same reference written on 28 June, Sholto Douglas said *"The C-in-C [i.e. himself] opposes the proposal to hand over the Ayr [Scotland] sector to the Americans. The Ayr sector is a very important one from the night-fighter point of view. The Americans know nothing about night fighting and it is doubtful if they will have any night fighters to begin with. For these reasons it is insisted that Ayr sector must remain British, ...although*

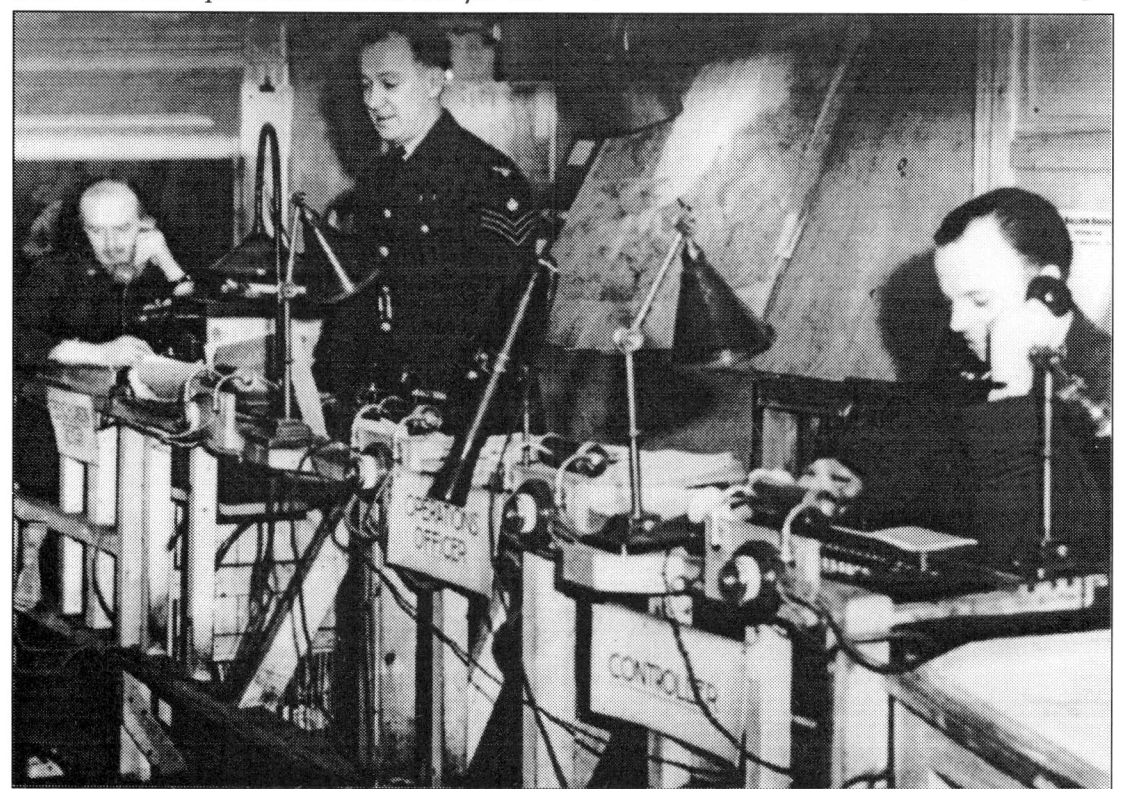

Another view of the temporary Operations Room in the Ballroom at Bentley Priory, showing the Controller and Operations Officers desks. The rough and ready nature of the structure is easily discernable.

there is no objection to having one US squadron there. It is suggested that a better plan would be to let the Americans take over the Andreas [Isle of Man] sector. It is convenient geographically to the Northern Ireland Group and is in a sense the outpost of the defence of Northern Ireland". The RAF airfield at Ayr had opened as recently as April 1941, but Andreas was still under construction, not becoming operational until October 1941.

Invasion fears

Fears of an impending invasion of Great Britain persisted, and in August 1941 Sholto Douglas issued a statement to the effect that he considered, broadly speaking, that the invasion threat was greatest along the coastline between the Wash and Newhaven in Sussex. Certain airfields, such as Martlesham Heath (Suffolk), Manston, Hawkinge and Lympne (all in Kent), might quickly become untenable, he believed, and he accepted that withdrawal of fighter squadrons from these Stations would have to be carried out rapidly should the need arise.

By now a corporal, Harold Gross attended a local course in anti-invasion tactics in 1941, during which an exercise was held in which he had to lead troops, all of whom were captured! Those taking part were told that Germans had landed; in fact they were Irish Guards, who quickly took control of the whole Station!

Air Cdre. Pearson recalls in his autobiography that in August 1941 the efforts of Ops.3 and the expanding night-fighter force began to have an effect on the Luftwaffe, although he says that the RAF squadrons never reached the critical ten percent attrition rate which had been sought. During that month, Air Cdre. Orlebar was promoted to AVM and was succeeded by Air Cdre. William Elliot.

Whether invasion was on the cards or not, the flow of important visitors to Bentley Priory continued. On 1 August the Director of the WAAF, Air Commandant J. Trefusis Forbes CBE, came to ensure that the girls under her command were being looked after, and next day AVM Goble of the Royal Australian Air Force arrived. 13 August was when the AOC-in-C showed the operations complex to Mr. John Wynant, who had succeeded the anti-British Joseph Kennedy as US Ambassador to the United Kingdom. On 18 August Prince Bernhardt of the Netherlands was seen, and two days later AVM Janouschek of the Czechoslovakian Air Force visited. A gentleman who had a great vested interest in the fast-developing RDF was its early pioneer, Dr. Robert Watson Watt, who came to Bentley Priory on 10 September.

During the night of 7/8 September 1941 a failing of the RDF system came to light when Ramsgate, Dover and Margate were bombed before a warning could be sounded. This came about when enemy bombers merged with streams of our own aircraft returning from a raid, thus being unidentifiable on the operations rooms' plotting tables.

The AOC-in-C and Lady Douglas had the enjoyable task on 22 October of inspecting six mobile canteens which were in the charge of a Mr. W. A. Thorne. Part of a consignment of 22 such vehicles, the canteens had been presented to Fighter Command by Mr. Cruger, the representative in the United Kingdom of the British War Relief Society of the USA.

Official policy concerning barrage balloons was the subject of a memorandum sent by Sholto Douglas to Air Ministry on 15 November 1941. In it, he stated that the importance of reducing the number of RAF aircraft damaged or brought down by our balloons was fully understood, and in the

Bentley Priory Strength - February 1942

	Officers	O/R	Total
RAF	397	894	1291
WAAF	68	1052	1120
Royal Navy	9	7	16
Royal Corps. of Signals	1	73	74
HQ Anti-Aircraft Cmnd	103	160	263
337th LL Batt. RA	4	44	48
4th Co. Trg. Bn. Irish Gds.	3	272	275
12th Cy. of London Co. ATS	3	67	70
FANY		15	15
Total	**588**	**2584**	**3172**

THE WAR YEARS

period of comparative inactivity by enemy aircraft then being enjoyed it should be possible to close-haul [i.e. tether at low level] the balloons without much risk. In fact balloons were already being close-hauled due to their proximity to the number of new airfields being opened. However, the sight of barrage balloons on the ground could affect public morale. It was essential, the AOC-in-C concluded, that adequate warning of attack be given.

Not of immediate significance to those at Bentley Priory was the entry of the United States of America into the war in Europe on 11 December 1941, when Hitler declared war on the USA. This event would, of course, have considerable effects on the outcome of hostilities as time went by, but for the time being Fighter Command was gathering strength for the offensive to come. During the previous month the Filter Room personnel had moved to the emergency room at Leighton Buzzard while alterations at Bentley Priory took place.

1942 began with the threat of invasion still hanging over Great Britain, and a decree that all fighter pilots were to be trained in action against invasion barges. So that pilots could become acquainted with beaches on which invading troops might land, lists were prepared by Fighter Command and sent to all Groups early in March.

Outside working hours, however, the community spirit among the residents of RAF Bentley Priory was maintained. On 28 February the Station Band gave a performance at Bushey Hall during a Special Warship Week concert, and next day members of the RAF and WAAF took part in a grand procession as part of Hemel Hempstead Warship Week.

The group of RAF men who had been involved in Station defence since April 1940 was organised as 713 Sqn. on 19 December 1941, and on the formation of the RAF Regiment on 1 February 1942 became fully-fledged as 2713 (Rifle) Sqn. Nevertheless, Army troops continued to come and go, and by the beginning of July 1942 the 30th Middlesex Regt., comprising five officers and 280 men, were present, as was the 451st LAA Battery. The girls of the City of London Company of the ATS had given way to others who were attached to HQ AA Command.

A first batch of ten officers of the USAAF arrived for tuition at the Controllers' Training Unit on 9 May 1942, and during the same month 66 RAF airmen reported for tests to decide their suitability for commissioning as Sector Controllers. Of their number, 39 were selected.

Sholto Douglas was promoted to Air Chief Marshal on a temporary basis at the end of June 1942. Two days earlier, the WAAFs had marched past when he took the salute on the third anniversary of the formation of the WAAF. Another parade, on 2 August, was held at Bushey Hall to mark the presentation of a mobile canteen to the County of Hertford, but by whom is not recorded. Yet another parade took place on 17 September, marking the second anniversary of the Battle of Britain, and on this occasion a message from the Commanding General of the USAAF was responded to by the Chief of the Air Staff, ACM Sir Charles Portal GCB DSO MC.

In September 1942 the men of 2713 (Rifle) Sqn. attended a battle training course at RAF Biggin Hill, where the squadron CO, Sqn. Ldr. Williams, had the misfortune to lose an eye in a nasty accident. Afterwards, No.3 Flight of the squadron went on a demonstration tour of all Fighter Command Stations.

Working in the 'hole' from September to November 1942 was Flt. Lt. (later Gp. Capt.) Hugh Verity, who moved from Uxbridge to Bentley Priory. During his own night-fighter course at Church Fenton in 1941, Hugh had almost been shot down by a Luftwaffe intruder, so when acting as an intruder controller at Bentley Priory he was gratified to be able to reciprocate, sending RAF aircraft to intrude at Luftwaffe bomber bases. The only equipment he and his colleagues used consisted of a small map table on which the enemy airfields were displayed and on which WAAFs moved plaques indicating

Fighter Command Order of Battle

April 1943

9 Group (HQ Barton Hall, Preston, Lancs.)
41	Spitfire	High Ercall
96	Beaufighter	Honiley
195	Typhoon	Woodvale
256	Mosquito	Woodvale
406	Beaufighter	Valley

10 Group (HQ Rudloe Manor, Bath)
312	Spitfire	Church Stanton
313	Spitfire	Church Stanton
175	Typhoon	Colerne
264	Mosquito	Colerne
266	Typhoon	Exeter
307	Mosquito	Exeter
310	Spitfire	Exeter
125	Beaufighter	Fairwood Common
412	Spitfire	Fairwood Common
193	Typhoon	Harrowbeer
504	Spitfire	Ibsley
616	Spitfire	Ibsley
164	Hurricane	Middle Wallop
456	Mosquito	Middle Wallop
65	Spitfire	Perranporth
141	Beaufighter	Predarmact
257	Typhoon	Warmwell
263	Whirlwind	Warmwell
184	Hurricane	Zeals

11 Group (HQ Uxbridge, Middlesex)
341	Spitfire	Biggin Hill
611	Spitfire	Biggin Hill
157	Mosquito	Bradwell Bay
132	Spitfire	Eastchurch
19	Spitfire	Fairlop
182	Typhoon	Fairlop
247	Typhoon	Fairlop
604	Beaufighter	Ford
183	Typhoon	Gatwick
174	Typhoon	Gravesend
245	Typhoon	Gravesend
91	Spitfire	Hawkinge
303	Spitfire	Heston
515	Defiant	Heston
122	Spitfire	Hornchurch
453	Spitfire	Hornchurch
3	Typhoon	Hunsdon
85	Mosquito	Hunsdon
129	Spitfire	Ibsley
403	Spitfire	Kenley
416	Spitfire	Kenley
181	Typhoon	Lasham
1	Typhoon	Lympne
131	Whirlwind	Manston
198	Typhoon	Manston
609	Typhoon	Manston
222	Spitfire	Martlesham Heath
421	Spitfire	Martlesham Heath
308	Spitfire	Northolt
315	Spitfire	Northolt
316	Spitfire	Northolt
124	Spitfire	North Weald
331	Spitfire	North Weald
332	Spitfire	North Weald
411	Spitfire	Redhill
197	Typhoon	Tangmere
486	Typhoon	Tangmere
485	Spitfire	Westhampnett
610	Spitfire	Westhampnett
29	Beaufighter	West Malling

12 Group (HQ Watnall, Notts)
25	Mosquito	Church Fenton
410	Mosquito	Coleby Grange
68	Beaufighter	Coltishall
118	Spitfire	Coltishall
402	Spitfire	Digby
306	Spitfire, Hurricane	Hutton Cranswick
302	Spitfire	Kirton-in-Lindsey
317	Spitfire	Kirton-in-Lindsey
56	Typhoon	Matlaske
151	Mosquito	Wittering

13 Group (HQ Ouston, Northumberland).
350	Spitfire	Acklington
409	Beaufighter	Acklington
64	Spitfire	Ayr
488	Beaufighter	Ayr
401	Spitfire	Catterick
130	Spitfire	Drem
219	Beaufighter	Scorton
340	Spitfire	Turnhouse

14 Group (HQ Drummossie Hotel, Inverness)
131	Spitfire	Castletown
165	Spitfire	Peterhead
66	Spitfire	Skaebrae
234	Spitfire	Skaebrae

RAF Northern Ireland
501	Spitfire	Ballyhalbert

THE WAR YEARS

The menacingly sleek shape of the De Havilland Mosquito Mk.II fight-fighter. The pair of 'pencils' sticking through the wing-tips are part of the radar system. [Winged Memories/BAe]

movements of Allied and hostile aircraft. With the aid of early warning from the 'Y' Service, the controller hoped to be able to arrange for Luftwaffe bases to be patrolled at the time the bombers were taking off, or failing that, when they were returning after raiding the UK. One night a raid on the north-east of England was plotted in and out, but no enemy aircraft were shot down by 13 Group pilots. Hugh Verity remarked to his 'Y' Service contact *"I'll bet you sixpence that Johnny Topham was not on tonight — I'm sure he'd have got one if he had been."* "OK, but how do we find out?" was the reply. Through 13 Group operations room, they telephoned the squadron dispersal and asked. Next day, Sholto Douglas summoned Hugh to his office to 'tear him off a strip'. The 13 Group AOC had complained that a member of Fighter Command staff had telephoned during the night to enquire why 13 Group had not shot down any enemy bombers. In November, Hugh Verity found himself posted to 161 (Special Duties) Sqn., flying secret agents to occupied France in Lysanders.

During September, the WAAF Sick Quarters was moved into *'Highfields'* in Magpie Hall Road, where space allowed for 22 beds instead of the 14 in the previous premises, 78 Bushey High Road. Another building requisitioned at this time was *'The Dearne'* in Uxbridge Road, Stanmore, into which eighty airmen of the CTU were able to move in October. On 1 October the Filter Room staff took up their possessions and moved once more to Leighton Buzzard to enable modifications to be made at Bentley Priory to cope with inland reporting, a task not previously necessary. However, due to lack of a plotting table and associated equipment, the project was suspended until the following March at the earliest.

A new AOC-in-C

Replacing Sholto Douglas, AM Sir Trafford Leigh-Mallory KCB DSO took over as AOC-in-C Fighter Command in November 1942, with AVM Callaway continuing in the post of Senior Air Staff Officer. Commandant of the HQ Unit was Wg. Cdr. J. B. Newman MBE.

Work on rebuilding the RAF Sick Quarters began in the early months of 1943 and made slow progress. All in-patients had to be transferred to neighbouring RAF Stations or to civilian hospitals while the work was carried out. By June the task was almost finished, with a new ward and treatment room in use. To provide for special dietary requirements, six hens were brought into service! Whether they were obliged to join the WAAF is not recorded.

With a message for Sir Kingsley Wood initiating Fighter Command's own Wings for Victory Week ringing in their ears, the personnel at Bentley Priory set about raising money on 17 May. By 26 May the campaign had raised £52,537 in Fighter Command as a whole, with Bentley Priory's total recorded at over £20,000,

RAF BENTLEY PRIORY AND STANMORE PARK

Bentley Priory Strength - December 1943

	Officers	O/R	Total
RAF in ADGB	389	509	898
RAF in AEAF	95	107	202
RAF in CTU	15	140	155
RAF in 5003 Works Flt.		64	64
RAF Regt. 2718 Sqn. det.	2	61	63
Allied staff in ADGB	29	12	41
Allied staff in AEAF		2	2
WAAF in ADGB	89	1315	1404
WAAF in AEAF	9	147	156
WAAF in CTU		3	3
HQ AA Command	125	121	246
ATS in HQ AA Command	6	245	251
371 LAA Battery RA	1	10	11
Royal Navy		13	13
Totals	**776**	**2733**	**3509**

though that seems a highly unlikely figure at about £7 per head, several weeks' wages for the average airman or WAAF.

After there had been a number of problems concerning movements of US 8th Air Force aircraft, Fighter Command suggested to its American equivalent on 10 June 1943 that US fighter squadrons should be instructed to notify the estimated time of departure and/or arrival of any aircraft to the Sector Operations Room within the area in which the airfield of departure was located. This information would be passed to Group Operations Rooms to enable the aircraft to be directed to the coast for handing over to the RDF operators. This move had been found necessary to cope with the increased number of offensive missions being flown by USAAF and RAF fighters. Another radical event took place on 13 July, when Fighter Command offered to provide a number of WAAFs to man GCI Stations on a temporary basis in order to judge their capability.

On 30 June 1943 Army Cooperation Command and 2 Group of Bomber Command were absorbed by Fighter Command. The Senior Engineering Staff Officer at HQ Fighter Command was then upgraded to Air Commodore rank and the post was filled by Air Cdre. Sutton-Jones, with Gp. Capt. Charleson, formerly with Army Cooperation Command, as his deputy. Much reallocation of duties had to be arranged to cope with the extra RAF Stations, about fifty in number, which were thus absorbed into Fighter Command. In addition, preliminary work on the setting-up of a tactical air force HQ, known as Allied Expeditionary Air Force (AEAF), in readiness for a forthcoming invasion of occupied Europe was carried out at Bentley Priory from October 1943. In command of the new organisation was ACM Leigh-Mallory, who transferred from Fighter Command.

After three and a half years at Bentley Priory in one form or another, 2713 (Rifle) Sqn. left in September 1943 to become the nucleus of the RAF Regiment Battle School at High Wycombe. During its time at the Priory 2713 Sqn. had, apart from its routine duties, provided guards of honour for such visiting dignitaries as King Haakon of Norway, King George of Greece, King Peter of Yugoslavia, Prince Bernhardt of the Netherlands, Gen. Eisenhower, General Montgomery, Gen. Giraud and Mrs Eleanor Roosevelt.

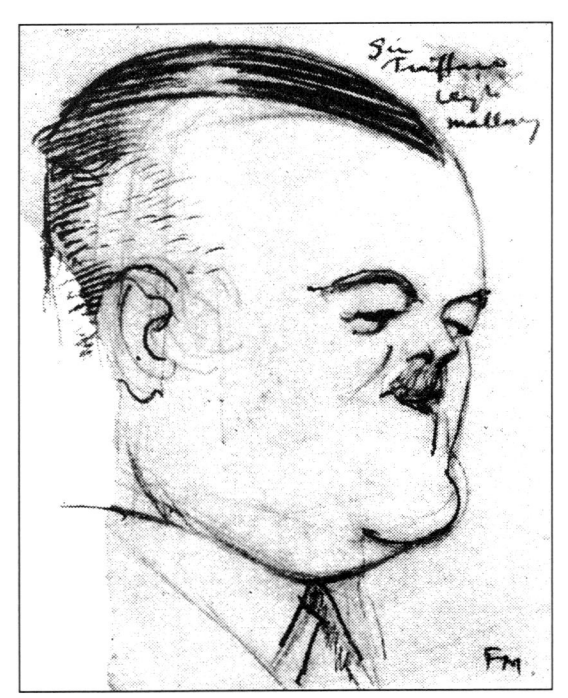

Major Fred May's pencil sketch of Sir Trafford Leigh-Mallory. [via Phillip May]

THE WAR YEARS

Known to some as 'Gremlin Castle', Stanmore Hall, in Wood Lane, off Stanmore Hill, was requisitioned as a Mess and accommodation for ninety officers working for the Allied Expeditionary Air Force in 1943/44. [AVM 'Sandy' Johnstone]

Squadron personnel had also formed the RAF Regiment detachment at the first Battle of Britain parade in London.

Allied Expeditionary Air Force
With ACM Sir Trafford Leigh-Mallory as its AOC-in-C, AEAF was formed on 15 November 1943 at *'Kestrel Grove'* in Hive Road, close to Bentley Priory. Second in command was an American, Maj. Gen. William D. Butler. Senior Air Staff Officer (SASO) was AVM H. E. Wigglesworth CB CBE DSC, while CO of the HQ unit and Camp Commandant was Flt. Lt. H. G. Cordiner. A War Room was established at Bentley Priory in the charge of Wg. Cdr. (soon Gp. Capt.) J. E. McComb and staffed by two RAF Gp. Capts. and two USAAF Colonels. For planning purposes, maps, aircraft serviceability boards, target photographs, weather reports and other aids were provided. A staircase was built, cutting through the floor of the War Room into the Battle Room, where day-to-day operations were displayed on a table connected to the ADGB equivalent. The British element of AEAF was created largely from former Fighter Command HQ staff, and there was a strong element of USAAF personnel. Part of the AEAF organisation was an Air Information Branch, set up specifically to make photographic records, including movie films, of the forthcoming invasion of Europe. Another section dealt with anticipated flying control problems, and included the preparation of common directives for the operation of the airstrips which would be built hastily in Normandy. Before long, 29 British and Dominion correspondents had been assigned to the Branch to cover air operations overseas and 33 to report from the Advanced Landing Grounds in Kent and Sussex before moving to France.

At the same time, Fighter Command was disbanded and in its place a new organisation known as Air Defence of Great Britain took over, under the direct control of AEAF. Placed in command of ADGB was Air Marshal Sir Roderic Hill CB MC AFC, whose SASO was AVM

Gen. Dwight D. Eisenhower, ACM Sir Trafford Leigh-Mallory, ACM Sir Arthur Tedder and other high-ranking officers exude an air of confidence as they study operational details of the forthcoming invasion of Europe at Bentley Priory. Photograph taken on 27 January 1944. [Crown Copyright via RAF Bentley Priory]

Callaway, who transferred from the old Fighter Command.

Extensions to the *'Woodlands'* premises used by CTU, comprising a third Synthetic Operations Room and two lecture huts, began in January 1944 and were completed in February. An acute shortage of staff had become a problem at the time, and another difficulty was the destruction of eight billet huts used by CTU when bombs fell in Elms Road, Harrow Weald on 19 February. Luckily nobody was injured. Accommodation for AEAF personnel was also difficult, but a dilapidated house known as *'The Rookery'* was taken over in February for use by WAAFs and WAACs. AEAF HQ was also experiencing space shortages, and in January in a field next to *'Kestrel Grove'* twelve marquees were erected and equipped with furniture, telephones and, perhaps, some form of heating!

With the number of people working at and around Bentley Priory so large, it was possible to stage high-quality entertainments outside working hours. On 6 February 1944, for instance, an All Star Show attended by the AOC-in-Cs of both ADGB and AEAF featured comedienne 'Two-ton' Tessie O'Shea, actor John Mills, singer Gwen Catley and 'heart-throb' actor Stewart Grainger, who no doubt was the subject of close scrutiny by most of the WAAFs present! In May the first issue of Bentley Priory Bulletin, containing details of forthcoming sporting events and entertainments, appeared.

Not so enjoyable was the enforced

THE WAR YEARS

ACM Sir Trafford Leigh-Mallory strolling through the Bentley Priory grounds in company with Field Marshal Smuts of South Africa, on 21 October 1943. [Crown Copyright via RAF Bentley Priory]

vaccination on 15 March of everyone on the Station against smallpox, which was prevalent locally. This measure, although painful ensured that no service personnel were affected.

In March 1944 ADGB, and therefore Bentley Priory, took on the responsibility for the twenty-four Advanced Landing Grounds which had been, or were still being, built in Kent, Sussex and Hampshire for use by fighter squadrons in the forthcoming invasion of Europe. This was also the month when stocks of equipment and supplies in connection with the invasion began arriving at Stations controlled by ADGB.

For the first time, a full-time padre was appointed on 10 May 1944 to look after the spiritual well-being of the personnel of ADGB, AEAF and Transport Command, which at the time was headquartered at Bush House in London. The gentleman involved, a member of the Church of England, was Sqn. Ldr. the Rev. Douglas A. Clarke.

Another American, Maj. Gen. Hoyt S. Vandenburg, took over from Maj. Gen. Butler as deputy commander of AEAF on 20 April 1944. In later years, Vandenburg was honoured by the naming of an air base in California after him. During May 1944, two visits to Bentley Priory were made by Lt. Col. Jacobs and Maj. Matthews of SHAEF to secure office accommodation for the Supreme Commander, Gen. Eisenhower, and his staff.

Movement among Station defence personnel were frequent during the build-up to D-Day. 2747 Sqn. RAF Regiment, which had replaced the AA Flight of 2718 Sqn. in April, departed in May.

Accommodation for students of CTU had become very difficult to find by May 1944, and many students were obliged to live in hostels in London, commuting to 'Woodlands' each day. Surprisingly, time was found to develop a unit garden, which by 1944 was producing a variety of food, including grapes, and which was the home of eight pigs and fifteen ducks! Close to 'Woodlands' was the 'tricycling field', on which airmen rode former Walls' ice cream trikes to simulate hostile aircraft for the benefit of trainee fighter controllers, at first being directed through loudspeakers placed around the field. This system had two disadvantages — the sound was heard clearly by local residents, and trainees could cheat by lifting their headphones from their ears and listening to the instructions! By June 1944 'walkie-talkie' two-way radios were in use, overcoming both problems.

Bentley Priory airstrip
In order to speed up communications within the embryo AEAF, it was felt that it would a great help if light aircraft such as Austers could be used by high-ranking staff officers. To take full advantage of this, a landing strip at Bentley Priory would be desirable, but ACM Leigh-Mallory did not approve of such measures. However, Gp. Capt. 'Batchy' Atcherley, talking in a London club to a US Army Colonel who commanded a road-building

RAF BENTLEY PRIORY AND STANMORE PARK

RAF Bentley Priory is seen from the north-west in this 1944 picture. Huts built as offices for use by the large number of personnel stationed at Bentley Priory are in the foreground; all have since been demolished and replaced by modern buildings closer to the Priory. In the top left-hand corner the two short-lived landing-strips for light aircraft can be seen, the east/west strip perilously close to the Priory building. [AVM 'Sandy' Johnstone]

unit, mentioned the idea to him. The response was, in effect, *"Let's get on with it!"*. On a Sunday soon afterwards, trees were cleared and two landing strips in the form of a T were soon usable. Both strips were short - the north/south strip was 870 feet (265m.) long and the east/west strip was only 390 feet (119m.) long! Leigh-Mallory was most unhappy, and seems to have done his best to minimise the use of the new facility. On 14 May the GOC-in-C of AA Command was notified *"On the subject of the landing strip... ...flying facilities are extremely restricted and were provided purely as an emergency measure for use of the Supreme Commander, the AOC-in-C and his senior staff officers when saving time is of direct importance to operations. For the present it is not possible to use the airstrip for the convenience of normal staff and Command visitors"*. A hangar was built on the north side for two Auster and one Vigilant light aircraft detached from the AEAF Communications Flight at Heston, and a few staff pilots were based at Bentley Priory. To complete this miniature airfield, a sergeant airfield controller was posted in, one assumes with a mobile runway-caravan in which to carry out his duties. On 10 May 1944 Atcherley made a trial landing successfully, and regular flying began, the largest number of outbound flights in a day being eleven. The airstrip remained a bone of contention, however.

D-Day at last!

Personnel serving at Bentley Priory had been aware for some time that something big was about to happen. When, early in

THE WAR YEARS

An Auster Mk.1, typical of those which used the Bentley Priory airstrip in 1944/45. [via author]

A Vultee Vigilant Mk.I aircraft, HL430, identical to the one used by the AEAF at Bentley Priory airstrip (which is believed to have been HL431). The RAF was to have received 100 of this STOL type from the United States, but only four arrived, the remainder being cancelled. [via R. C. Sturtivant]

the morning of 6 June 1944, a very large number of aircraft flying at low level in the direction of France were seen and the 08.00 radio news broadcast was heard everyone knew that the liberation of Europe was under way. D-Day had arrived at last! Although Bentley Priory was the headquarters of ADGB and AEAF, the secret was very well kept, and no information leaked out. During the morning, excitement grew. At 11.00 ACM Hill read Eisenhower's Order of the Day over the Tannoy loudspeaker system and a transcript of the speech was given later to all personnel. In the afternoon, HM the King, the Prime Minister and Field Marshall Smuts visited the War Room to see what progress was being made.

A further branch of AEAF, known as CATOR (Combined Air Transport Operations Room), had been organised in April and May 1944 to act as the nerve centre for air transport services following the invasion, under the command of Gp. Capt. Ralph Bagby. Seven USAAF and five RAF officers maintained a 24-hour watch, controlling ten RAF and USAAF airfields and the squadrons based on them.

Operations began on D-Day minus 1, when supplies were dropped to troops who had parachuted into Normandy before the seaborne assault. As soon as airstrips were available 'on the far shore', aircraft under CATOR control began landing to deliver cargoes of K-rations, blood plasma, equipment and other vital requirements and to uplift wounded troops. In July, a scheduled service for freight and passengers was started, and by the end of the month 34,492 injured men had been evacuated to hospitals in England and 9675 tonnes of cargo delivered. In addition, VIPs and other members of the forces were flown to France, and CATOR also controlled the Air Delivery Letter Service, flown three times a day by Hurricanes.

D-Day or not, social and sporting activities continued to occupy the spare time of the RAF and WAAFs at Bentley Priory. Just before the big day, on 3 June, the Station was represented at the local 'Salute The Soldier' parade at Bushey by fifty WAAFs under the command of Flt. Off. McNab, with Wt. Off. Mayes MBE acting as parade marshall. The girls were probably fitter than ever, as all ranks

RAF BENTLEY PRIORY AND STANMORE PARK

Posing on the steps at the rear of the Priory in 1944, when the Allied Expeditionary Air Force had its headquarters there, were (l. to r.) ACM Sir Arthur Tedder (Deputy Supreme Allied Commander); Maj. Gen. William D. Butler USAAF; Gen. Dwight D. Eisenhower (Supreme Allied Commander); and ACM Sir Trafford Leigh-Mallory (C-in-C AEAF). The presence of these 'top brass' officers indicates the vital work being carried out at Bentley Priory at the time. [Crown Copyright via RAF Bentley Priory]

under the rank of Flt. Sgt. had since 15 May been obliged to take part in at least one period of PT every week. The same girls, perhaps, took part in pouring rain in a parade on 28 June marking the fifth anniversary of the formation of the WAAF. This time, 40 officers and 400 WAAFs were addressed by the ADGB AOC-in-C, who congratulated them on their bearing and mentioned that it was likely that WAAFs would soon be sent to serve across the Channel. A special lunch which followed included strawberries and cream. During the evening a cocktail party was held by the officers at No.1 Mess *('Barlogan')* and there was a Station dance. Afterwards, messages of congratulation were received from HRH the Duchess of Gloucester (Air Commandant of the WAAF), AM Sir Charles Portal GCB DSO CB (Chief of the Air Staff) and the AOC-in-C. Within two days, a large number of WAAFs volunteered for service with AEAF on the Continent and were interviewed, though how many were accepted is not recorded.

The only accident known to have taken place on the Bentley Priory airstrip occured on 14 June 1944, when Auster Mk.V MT356 of the AEAF Communications Sqn. overturned while landing. Some reports say that 'Batchy' Atcherley was flying the aircraft, others that Lt. Bennett of the USAAF was the pilot. Damage was only slight, and the Auster survived to fly again after repairs. Other aircraft using the strip included L-5 Sentinels of the USAAF bringing documents to AEAF headquarters and L-4 Cubs with American medical personnel. From 6 June ACM Sir Arthur Harris, AOC-in-C of Bomber Command, was a visitor almost daily. Gen. Eisenhower and a number of other Allied air commanders who visited the Priory on 31 May, and Generals 'Toohey' Spaatz and Doolitle, who arrived on 3 June, may well have touched down on the airstrip.

'Doodlebugs' menace!

Flying bombs, Hitler's dreaded V1 secret weapon, better known as 'buzz-bombs' or 'doodlebugs', now began to make themselves felt. On 21 June an order was issued to warn personnel not to discuss this 'terror' weapon, which was harassing southern England. Difficulties in dealing with the V1s were outlined on 29 July by

THE WAR YEARS

A V1 flying bomb - 'Vergeltungswaffe, or reprisal weapon number one' was known by the populace as the 'doodlebug'. Containing 850 kilos of high explosive, the pilotless bomb was a real menace. The example shown here was displayed on a section of its launching ramp at the Science Museum in London at the end of the war.

ADGB, which stated that to provide proper coverage of the London area by searchlights in order to warn civilians it would be necessary to double the number of lights. Ironically, that very day and next day, V1s fell about a mile from Bentley Priory, near Oxhey crossroads. V1s did not always keep to a straight course and flew at low altitudes, and there was a problem of finding enough sites for searchlights on high ground. Another feature of the campaign against V1s was the redeployment of a large number of balloon squadrons and their personnel across south-east England. However, the new Gloster Meteor jet fighter aircraft was just coming into service, and in due course proved an effective remedy. The ROC was prominent in identifying and tracking the V1s across south-east England, and no case is known of a 'buzz-bomb' arriving without being correctly identified. By this time, when so many Allied aircraft were airborne over the Channel, the function of the ROC had become even more important. At the same time, it was found necessary to improve low-level radar cover in the area in which the V1s were flying, and a microwave early warning (MEW) radar set borrowed from the United States was put into service at Fairlight in Sussex, linked to Horsham and Maidstone ROC Centres. In the two months that the MEW was in use, it was able to direct the destruction of no less than 142 'buzz-bombs'.

It was noted in June 1944 that attendance at sick parades of Bentley Priory personnel had increased, and this was considered to be due in part to general war weariness aggravated by a lack of leave time. When 'doodle-bugs' began to pass within earshot of the Priory, a casualty clearing scheme was brought back into action, consisting of two first aid teams led by qualified medical officers and equipped with ambulances. They could be sent to any part of the Station at short notice without having an adverse effect on

Gloster Meteor Mk 1 EE223 YQ:Y of 616 Squadron as used to intercept the V1's [via R Sturtivant]

RAF BENTLEY PRIORY AND STANMORE PARK

the SSQ. A contributing factor to the degree of illness may have been the food in the airmen's mess, which according to Harold Gross, by then a Flt. Sgt. working on light duties due to his own indifferent health, was *"awful"*. As orderly sergeant one day, he made a formal complaint to the Station Adjutant, Sqn. Ldr. Seymour, whose response was to ask him whether he wanted a posting to Singapore!

Glenn Miller at the Priory

At Bentley Priory the NAAFI re-opened on 20 July 1944 after refurbishment and redecoration. To celebrate the event, ENSA provided a concert by Alfredo & His Band, a type of entertainment said to be much appreciated by the 'troops'. A week later, the 'Bentley Players' staged their first production, the thriller 'Night Must Fall', by Emlyn Williams. By far the most exciting performance seen and heard at Bentley Priory so far, however, was the concert given on 16 August 1944 by the already-famous Glenn Miller and his AEAF Band. Glenn and his musicians had performed at the massive USAAF Base Air Depot at Burtonwood in Lancashire the previous day, and had then flown to Twinwood Farm airfield, near the band's base at Bedford. Next day a C-47 transport aircraft flew Glenn, Col. Ed Kirby (Director of Troop Broadcasting) and Lt. Don Haynes, the band's executive officer, to Hendon, where a potentially fatal accident was just averted. On final approach the C-47 narrowly avoided a B-17 Fortress aircraft which was already on the runway, and the pilot was obliged to abort the landing and make another attempt. The full forty-piece band, meanwhile, made the journey to Bentley Priory in road transport.

The performance took place in the open air, on the grass area which faces the main entrance to the Priory building. According to the diary kept by Ed Kirby, a V.1 'doodlebug' flew within sight of the Priory during the concert, and on hearing it the players lowered the sound level until Glenn, conducting the band, was sure that the V.1 had passed by. This event was re-enacted with a great deal of artistic licence in the film 'The Glenn Miller Story' in a scene in which the V.1 flies almost overhead and a number of wounded personnel are visible, neither of which applied to the Bentley Priory concert. The building used in the movie was nothing like the Priory and was in fact a children's home in Denver, Colorado!

Among the thousand or so service personnel who watched and listened to Glenn and his music was LACW Ida Goodwin, a cook, who during the interval approached the great man and asked for his autograph, only to be given a refusal, because, they were told that *"If I give it to you I'll have to give it to everyone"*. Afterwards, Ida and her friend June Sheppard found that Glenn had indeed given his autograph to many people, but not to them! After the performance, Glenn and his men left to make a recording to be

Maj. Glen Miller (2nd right) with other members of the AEAF Band , seen here ar Bedford in November 1944. [Art Nanas via Martin Bowman]

THE WAR YEARS

broadcast later. Four months later, Glenn Miller disappeared between England and France in circumstances which remain mysterious to this day.

More accommodation for AEAF personnel soon became needed, and on 25 July 1944 *'Gooden Gate'* in Stanmore Hill was requisitioned as a WAAF hostel and *'East Haddon,* (recorded in the ORB as *East Haven)* also in Stanmore Hill, became a WAAF officers' quarter. Little St. Margaret's School at Bushey was taken over as accommodation for forty personnel.

With the advent of AEAF, a vastly increased amount of signals traffic had been experienced. On 31 July, the signals facilities used by ADGB and AEAF were combined in order to simplify the proceedings. Teleprinters were moved from the Operations and Intelligence rooms to three new huts above ground, the W/T organisation expanded to fill a large Nissen hut next to the teleprinter huts and another hut was occupied by an enlarged Intelligence section. Thus in six months the Signals Section had expanded from one hut to two standard Nissens, one 72-foot (22m.) Nissen and three smaller huts, while yet another Nissen hut was being built. At Hill House a Nissen to accommodate the W/T section was being erected. At much the same time, a large hut was taken over at Garston, near Watford, to form a transmitting station, and an adjacent field was requisitioned to house mobile W/T equipment. In terms of personnel, the Signals Section had grown from one officer and 219 other ranks to five officers and 390 other ranks. Housing for WAAFs employed on signals work then became a problem, and billets at Elstree formerly used by the army were taken over. For Filter Room staff, two more premises on Stanmore Hill, 'Woodlands' and 2 Halsbury Close, were requisitioned in August 1944, as was *'East Haddon'* at Elstree, which was to be used by WAAF officers. Use of these premises posed the never-ending problems of transport and messing arrangements.

As the front line in France moved forward, the time came for AEAF to leave England for a new location nearer the action. On 20 August 1944 a Forward unit left *'Kestrel Grove'* on its way to Eastleigh, near Southampton, before making the Channel crossing to Granville in Normandy. Operation 'Market Garden', the large-scale but disastrous drop of parachutists in the Arnhem area of Holland, was a major project handled from the War Room at AEAF headquarters, which acted as the link between AEAF (Rear) and the 2nd TAF on the Continent from 17 to 23 September 1944. Rear Headquarters remained in place until disbanding on 15 October 1944, on which date RAF Kestrel Grove was formed with the sole task of completing the winding-up of what had become SHAEF (Air) Rear, which included CATOR, by 15 December, though in fact this procedure took much longer. Completing the reorganisation, on 16 October ADGB reverted to its original title of Fighter Command. A general reorganisation of offices then took place, and at the same time 4699 Works Flt., attached to Bentley Priory for the purpose, began work on an extension

Also used to counter the V1 menace were Hawker Typhoons, this example being DN374, a Mk.1b of 56 Squadron. [via author]

to the Sergeants' Mess.

Kestrel Grove was handed back to HQ Fighter Command on 19 December for use by the Royal Observer Corps, and Flg. Off. Earl was appointed CO of the Bentley Priory detachment of SHAEF (Air) Rear, most of which had taken up residence in the former USAAF headquarters at Bushy Park, near Hampton Court. With his office in hut 64 at the Priory, Flg. Off. Earl was in charge of 89 officers, including eight WAAFs, 189 airmen and 145 airwomen. One hut in the grounds of *'Kestrel Grove'* was also used, but seven more huts there were now taken over by AA Command.

The largest aircraft ever to touch down on Bentley Priory's tiny airstrip did so on 21 September, when a C-64 Norseman of the USAAF made a precautionary landing in very poor weather. Its pilot managed to take off after the weather had cleared, much to the relief of the airfield controller. Other aircraft using the strip early in 1945 were a number of UC-61 Arguses of the USAAF, two of them from the Base Air Depot at Burtonwood in Lancashire.

Among all this activity, a new unit, 6 RAF Film Production Unit, was formed at Bentley Priory in October 1944 for service overseas, the stores at the Priory providing much of its equipment.

While some requisitioning was still taking place, other premises were released to their owners. Among them were five at Elstree — *'The Thistles'*, *'Duke Villa'*, *'Down Villa'*, *'Headmaster's House'* and *'St. Mary's Croft'*. During September, *'Goring'*, *'Hardwick'*, *'Kelso'*, *'Oaklands'* and 14 and 16 Marsh Lane were transferred from use by the departed AEAF so that they could be used by signals personnel, while *'Belmont'* came into use by Code & Cypher officers. Added to the students of CTU in September were sixteen West Indians. To avoid any problems of colour prejudice among local householders they slept in a lecture room, and were highly thought of by the CTU staff.

'Two Oaks', a property at Elstree which had been in use since early 1940, was de-requisitioned in November 1944,

Taken over as officers' quarters on the outbreak of war in 1939, 'County End' in Magpie Hall Road reverted to a private house at the end of 1944. [author]

continuing the trend. The AMWD, meanwhile, was busy repairing a number of buildings which had been neglected during the stressful years of the war. In the same month, the WAAF canteen closed but was immediately reopened by the YWCA for use throughout the 24 hours by service and civilian workers. In December, the armaments, photographic, equipment and engineering Sections moved from Cedars Close to other hutted accommodation. The Operational Research Section vacated *'Clodiagh'* and *'The Bowls'* in favour of huts on the Station itself. *'County End'*, which had served as No.2 Officers' Mess, was also vacated. Stanmore Hall, a large rambling building half way up Stanmore Hill, was returned to Fighter Command by SHAEF (Air) Rear in December, the occupants moving over the next few weeks to a smaller property in Hive Road known as *'Holmebury'*, which needed a great deal of redecoration. Stanmore Hall had been used before requisitioning as eight service flats, after which a staff of sixty looked after ninety officers who slept in single rooms and dormitories. Up to 270 lunches and 170 evening meals were provided during the building's RAF heyday. Even after the officers had left, Stanmore Hall was used to accommodate 35 WAAFs who moved out of *'The Rookery'* when it became uninhabitable due to a lack of water caused by burst pipes.

Work performed by the Signals Section in 27 days of November 1944 comprised 56,607 signals handled (a daily average of 2025), of which 21,092 were cross-Channel messages (752 per day on average). The average daily total of cypher groups handled was 32,328. Teleprinter line serviceability was 66.8%.

A measure designed to minimise the effect of the V1 flying bombs was taken by Signals Branch at Bentley Priory in December, when the Naval C-in-C Nore agreed to order his ships to report sightings of the 'doodle-bugs' on a certain radio frequency direct to the Filter Room, from where the information on bearing, course and height of the missile would be relayed to 11 Group Filter Room for positive action.

Taken seriously by the authorities in 1944 was an increase in the number of illegitimate pregnancies. In an effort to make the WAAFs more aware of the seriousness of what was coyly described as 'the act', Group officers were instructed to consider any WAAF officers who might be suitable for delivering the approved Air Ministry lecture on moral behaviour. Whether this had any effect on the spare-time activities of members of the RAF is not recorded!

With the end of the war in Europe within the Allies' grasp, 1945 began at Bentley Priory with the opening of the Cross-Channel Signals Centre on 7 January. One day was all that was necessary for the move of numerous personnel and pieces of equipment from Uxbridge, and Bentley Priory then became the main outlet for RAF communications to and from AEAF in Europe. A marked increase in the number of signals handled now developed. In January 82,388 signals were handled, a daily average of 2354. Cross-Channel signals totalled 42,028 (1201 per day on average), double the previous month's total. However, there was a continuous flow of officers away from the Station on postings overseas, and representations had to be made at the highest level in order to slow the exodus. Somewhat patronisingly, Signals Branch reported that WAAFs were *"just as good as men in routine circumstances, but in an emergency which had to be dealt with without fluster the men were superior"*. An enquiry had been received in connection with a Commission on equal pay which was then taking evidence.

There now seemed to be an end to the V1 flying bomb assault, but unfortunately the V2 rocket had begun to make itself felt. Far worse than the V1 because there was no warning of its approach, the V2 was invulnerable to defences. At 03.58 on 27 January 1945 one of these dreadful weapons fell in a field near Adelaide Close, Stanmore, about 800 yards from the premises used by the CTU. There and in the WAAF hostels many panes of glass were broken, but there were no injuries.

During January 1945 a Rear Element of 2 Group, which by then was on the Continent, was formed at Bentley Priory to control 136 and 140 Wings, and took up residence in the recently-vacated Cedars Close huts. With them was the HQ of Tactical Air Force (UK) Staff, headed by Wg. Cdr. F. A. Wray. Bushey Hall, which since 1943 had been used by the USAAF, was returned to the RAF on 15 February for administration by Bentley Priory staff. A great deal of effort went into removing equipment from the building, after which a Care & Maintenance Party remained there to ensure security. The Bentley Priory airstrip, no longer needed, was closed in February and the hangar dismantled.

To help the many WAAFs at Bentley Priory to settle back into the civilian life which would be theirs after demobilisation, a domestic science course began on 12 February at the signals section hostel at Elstree, with lessons by a Good Housekeeping instructor. Tuition was given in housewifery, laundry, cooking and sewing, and classes were sometimes held in a cottage decorated by the WAAFs.

Although the national fuel supply situation had become critical, arrangements were made for Bentley Priory to be given some form of priority to

RAF BENTLEY PRIORY AND STANMORE PARK

allow the mains heating system to continue to function. One assumes that the 65 players in a symphony orchestra conducted by Basil Cameron who played on an extended stage in the Station Theatre did not suffer the cold unduly!

Bushey Hall came back into use when it was occupied temporarily on 15 March 1945 by the Air Division of the Control Commission for Germany when that organisation was being formed. However, on 30 March a huge fire on the premises caused the loss of a great deal of equipment, and the south wing of the building was burnt out. Nevertheless, 103 (Disarmament) Wing, which had formed on 12 February 1945, took up residence there.

'Montrose', which had long served as the AOC-in-C's residence but had been unoccupied for several months, was transferred on 21 April to HQ 43 Group for use as single officers' quarters. Stanmore Hall, vacated in February by SHAEF (Rear), was re-occupied in April by WAAFs who moved out of the Prep. School at Bushey. Other empty buildings, *'Clodiagh'* and *'The Bowls'*, were brought back into use as No.4 WAAF Officers' Mess and accommodation. *'Haydon Hill'* and 78 Bushey High Road were vacated, while *'Otway Cottage'* and *'Colne View'*, which were occupied by 103 Wing staff, became the responsibility of Bentley Priory. In May, *'Pennimead'*, *'The Oaks'* and *'Homestead'*, all at Elstree, were vacated, and *'Whyteways'* and Perry's Garage, which were also in use by 103 Wing, were added to Bentley Priory's property portfolio.

The end of hostilities!

On 7 May 1945, Fighter Command HQ at Bentley Priory issued a General Cease Fire Order to all Groups under its command and to HQ AA Command. Nevertheless, a 'standby' order was in force until the threat of air attack was deemed to have passed. On VE Day, 8 May, all personnel other than those on essential duty were given total freedom to do whatever they wished, within reason of course! A service of thanksgiving was held in the chapel, after which there was a free issue of beer and minerals to all other ranks at lunchtime. In the evening there was a dance in the Station cinema, when beer was sold at 6d (2.5p.) per pint and there was a free buffet. Flt. Lt. Mackay, the Station entertainments officer, had decorated the cinema for the occasion, and the band was none other than the 'Skyrockets', under Sgt. Paul Fenhoulet. Weighing nearly 2 cwts. (100kg.), a Victory cake decorated with icing representing an airfield layout, had been made by the mess Warrant Officer and his staff. At 22.30, seven tons (7.12 tonnes) of waste material piled into a heap was lit and blazed away until nearly 03.00 next morning. Meanwhile, the AOC-in-C was entertained in the sergeants' mess. After all that, only one case of absenteeism was reported next morning!

A large parade of thanksgiving was held on 12 May on Priory Green, and ACM Sir Roderic Hill gave a farewell address to about a thousand service men and women on his appointment to a post on the Air Council. Providing the music were the bands of Fighter Command and the WAAF. So ended a long period of intense activity at RAF Bentley Priory. Now, under the command of AM Sir James Robb KCB CB DSO DFC AFC, a very different future was in store for Fighter Command. Personnel numbers had increased enormously over the six years of hostilities, and at the end of April no less than 3786 people were working at or around Bentley Priory. This number included 19 Czechs, 31 Poles, three members of the RNZAF, six RAAF, 13 RCAF, three Belgians and 11 members of the Royal Navy. Army personnel of HQ AA Command totalled 526, half of them girls of the ATS.

On the same day, the final aircraft plots were recorded by the members of the Royal Observer Corps and the whole ROC network closed down, after five and a half years of hard work of which the general public was largely unaware. After a number of celebration parades, the ROC organisation went onto a Care & Maintenance basis to await developments.

RAF BENTLEY PRIORY AND STANMORE PARK

Chapter Four

Fifty Years of Peace, 1945 to 1995

A return to routine
As soon as hostilities were over, a period of retrenchment of Fighter Command began, and much effort went into the procedures of airfield closure, redeployment and limited re-equipment with new Meteor and Vampire jet fighter aircraft. At Bentley Priory, demobilisation gathered pace, but it was possible to mount a contribution to the Victory Parade in London on 8 May, when one WAAF officer and fifteen other ranks took part. By December, personnel numbers had dropped to 748, of which 570 were RAF and only 178 WAAFs, and within a month the total had shrunk to 595. The service police section was in particular difficulties, no doubt to the quiet delight of the average serviceman or woman! Despite repeated requests, no additional staff had been added to the two corporals who manned the section, of which the established number of personnel was fifteen! All requisitioned property had been returned to its owners by the end of 1946.

After less than two years, the Royal Observer Corps was brought out of its period of Care & Maintenance in January 1947 at Bentley Priory. The Corps then took up its previous task of reporting aircraft movements, and now there were more fast jet fighters to deal with. At the time, no threat of war in the following ten years was seen — until the beginning of the Berlin Airlift in June 1948. Members of the ROC carried on with their well-practiced job, but in 1948 the AOC-in-C Fighter Command visited a number of Posts and was horrified to see the primitive conditions they endured. Protective clothing was then issued! Among those working at ROC HQ as a

A rear view of Bentley Priory about 1950; the wooden huts at the west end of the Italian garden have long since been removed, as can be seen in more recent pictures. [J. W. Tarrant]

RAF BENTLEY PRIORY AND STANMORE PARK

HRH the Duchess of Gloucester, in the uniform of an Air Chief Commandant, inspecting the WAAF contingent at Bentley Priory on the occasion of the eighth birthday of the WAAF, 28 June 1947. The LACW on the left of the picture is wearing a long-service stripe; perhaps she was one of the original members of the service. [Sqn. Ldr. Diana McCall WRAF (Retd.)]

teenage temporary civil servant was Mrs. Mavis Warrender, who recalls that the Commandant of the ROC at the time was Air Cdre. the Earl of Bandon, a kindly man who took pity on young Mavis when she slipped and dropped a tray of tea on the way to his office, providing a tot of Irish whiskey to help her recuperate.

A new unit, the Clerk/General Duties School, was formed on 6 February 1947 to train personnel of that trade in Fighter Command. An intake of forty per month was planned, and this caused a slight rise in the number of personnel at Bentley Priory. This was a time of acute fuel shortage, but large quantities of solid fuel were collected from other RAF Stations on the authority of the Air Ministry in order to maintain Fighter Command's effort.

Disaster struck the Priory at 22.45 on 10 March 1947, when a fire in an anteroom of the officers' mess was reported. Extensive damage, estimated at £15,000 to £20,000, was caused to office accommodation adjacent to and above the seat of the blaze. The National Fire Service dealt with the fire, in conditions of frost-bound snow, and next day a Court of Enquiry sat to consider the event.

Repairs to the Priory had been completed by the time the eighth birthday of the WAAF arrived on 28 June 1947. That sunny day at 12.30, Air Chief Commandant HRH the Duchess of Gloucester was received at Bentley Priory by the Director of the WAAF, Air Commandant Felicity Hanbury MBE, and Wing Officer M. E. Clancey. The Duchess inspected a guard of honour of 51 WAAFs of HQ Fighter Command led by Flt. Off. E. D. Coulthard MBE. Two Regional bands provided music at a lunch party held by ACM Robb and Lady Robb, during which a number of WAAF officers and airwomen were presented to the Duchess. After tea in the NAAFI, the Duchess left, and a

FIFTY YEARS OF PEACE

At Bentley Priory the candles on the birthday cake made to celebrate the eighth birthday of the WAAF were blown out by the oldest airwoman (a beribboned Flt. Sgt.) and the youngest...

Below: Air Chief Marshal Sir John Slessor and the Director of the WAAF, Air Commandant Dame Felicity Hanbury, look on while HRH the Duchess of Gloucester cuts the celebration cake at the WAAF eighth birthday party at Bentley Priory on 28 June 1947. [Sqn. Ldr. Diana McCall WRAF (Retd.)]

preview of a proposed new WAAF uniform was then held. All concerned agreed that the day had been a great success.

Total strength of personnel in June 1947 had, surprisingly, risen to 842, including 199 WAAFs and five prisoners of war. By November, staff of the London Air Traffic Control Centre (ATCC) were being accommodated at Bentley Priory and were taken by coach to their work at Uxbridge each day. That month, AVM Sir William Elliott KBE CB DFC inspected Fighter Command HQ on taking over as AOC-in-C from AM Sir James Robb. Befitting his position, Sir William received promotion to AM on 1 July 1948.

Staff numbers showed a steady decline in the early part of 1948, so that by June the total had fallen to 544, made up of 399 RAF and 145 WAAFs. Some of them were affected by a fire which damaged a large part of the roof of the airmen's mess on 27 May, started by long-term smouldering caused by the heat of a stack-pipe.

Just before a major exercise was held, Bentley Priory received a visit from His Imperial Majesty the Shah of Iran on 23 July 1948, and a guard of honour was presented to him. One of the WAAFs at Bentley Priory recalls the amount of 'bull' and feverish cleaning-up which had to be done before this visit, for which she was on parade. Shift workers, of whom there were many, could often contrive to miss such ceremonial activities, sometimes legally! The exercise, code-named 'Dagger', took place from 3 to 5 September and was designed to test the complete defences of Great Britain, with the RAF, the ROC and the USAF taking part. In the scenario, 'Southland' issued an ultimatum to 'Northland', expiring at midday on 3 September, exactly nine years after the opening of the Second World War. 'Southland's' forces included elements of Coastal, Transport and Flying Training Commands, RAF Germany and some Hornet aircraft of Fighter Command, plus the USAF in Europe, while 'Northland' mustered all front-line fighter squadrons of

RAF BENTLEY PRIORY AND STANMORE PARK

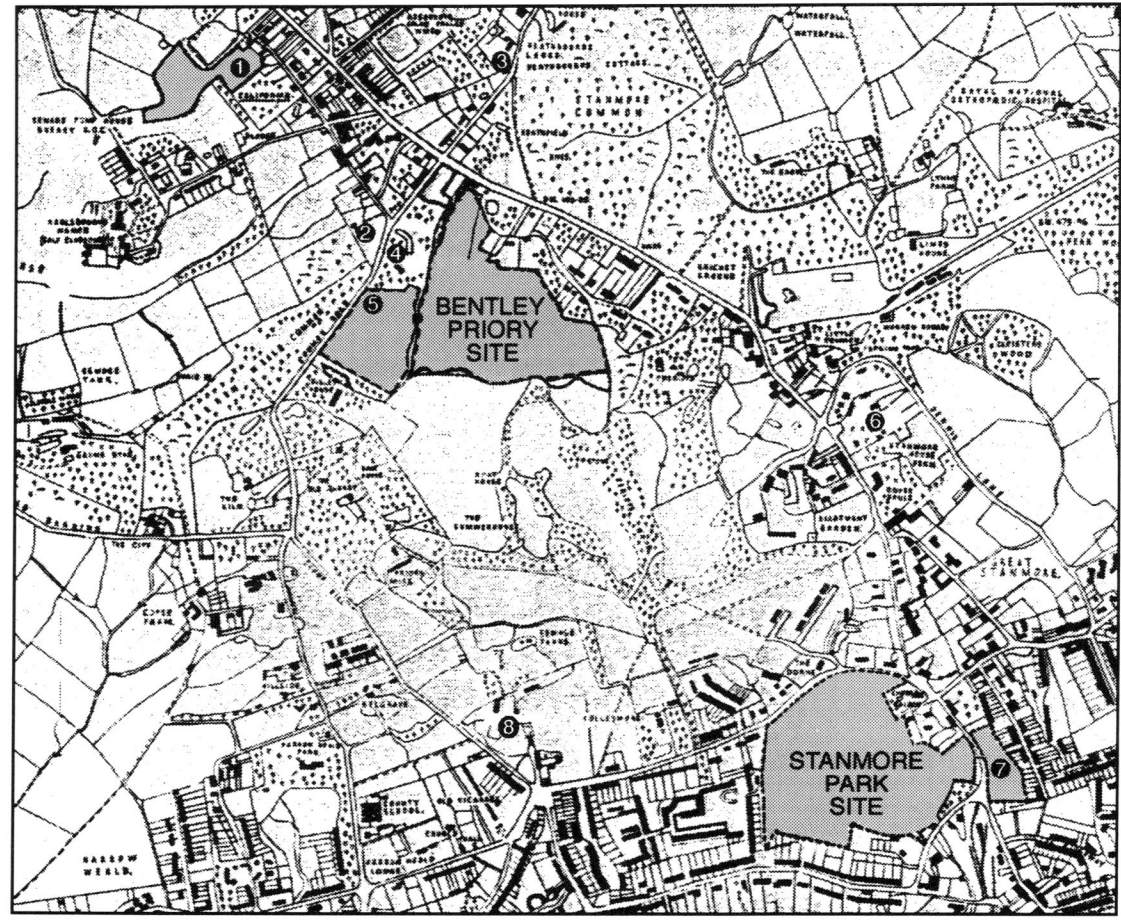

An area map showing the Bentley Priory and Stanmore Park sites, along with other requisitioned buildings and sites. 1- THE WARREN, 2 - KESTREL GROVE, 3- COUNTY END, 4- TANGLEWOOD, 5 - GLENTHORN, 6 - STANMORE HALL, 7 - MANOR HOUSE - 8 - WOODLAND.

the RAF except the Hornets, plus the RAuxAF, AA units, the ROC and the Control & Reporting System. All operations were controlled from Bentley Priory by the DCAS, AM Sir Hugh Walmsley, who afterwards complimented all concerned.

No sooner had the dust settled than another important visitor arrived at Bentley Priory — the Begum Liaquat Ali Khan, wife of the President of the recently-established state of Pakistan, who was accompanied by the wife of the High Commissioner of Pakistan and Air Commandant Felicity Hanbury. Their mission seems to have been to ensure the welfare of the WAAF, whose quarters and dining hall they visited.

Routine exercises with Bomber Command and the USAF continued in the last three months of 1948, and the somewhat ominous formation of a War Readiness Committee took place. On 15 November a ceremonial parade was held to commemorate the birth of Prince Charles.

Life at a peacetime Bentley Priory

Among the WAAFs who served at Bentley Priory in the late 1940s was Mrs. Eva Taylor, who says that her memories of the place are all happy ones. *"Everyone seemed to get along really well together, and the majority of us were so content with our lives in camp that we rarely wanted to*

FIFTY YEARS OF PEACE

go out in search of more entertaining activities. Whenever there was something special to celebrate - a birthday, an engagement or a posting, for instance - we would all trip off down to the village (as it truly was in those days!) and gather together in the back room of the Crown. Everyone donated to a 'kitty' which was handed over to the landlord, who then kept us supplied with jugs of beer and bits to eat until the cash ran out. By that time everyone had usually had enough and there would be a much less orderly procession back to camp!" One of the facilities was a games room frequented by a number of good table-tennis players. Quite often, very popular dances were arranged in the NAAFI, with a proper band providing the music. Bentley Priory is close enough to London for those who wanted to see the sights to travel there for the day by Underground, although, as always, 'other ranks' usually had little spare cash. *"Even if we had been paid a great deal better than we were"*, Eva Taylor remarks, *"it would have been difficult to spend much of it on luxury items such as chocolates or civilian clothes as these were still rationed. Because our generation had been brought up through the severe austerity conditions that prevailed during the war years, it had become second nature to make do with what little we had, and also to make our own entertainment to a large extent. This probably explains why the NAAFI was the focal point of our off-duty hours. People just sat around in there talking, and a lot of laughing and bantering and joking went on, and of course there was the piano with the inevitable sing-song taking place, and all sorts of card games and darts and so forth to join in. There were times that were harder than others — the few days before*

Air Marshal Sir Basil Embry KBE CB DSO DFC AFC, AOC-in-C Fighter Command, taking the salute at the King's Birthday parade at Bentley Priory in 1949. The position of the flagpole has not been altered since then. [J. W. Tarrant]

RAF BENTLEY PRIORY AND STANMORE PARK

This picture of Air Marshal Sir Basil Embry taking the salute at the 1949 parade in honour of the birthday of King George VI gives a good impression of the Priory building from the north-west. The two buildings on the left of the picture were wartime offices, since demolished. [J. W. Tarrant]

pay day, for instance, when everyone was flat broke. I can recall sharing one cup of coffee in the NAAFI between three of us, and one cigarette being passed around half a dozen of us during a night 'bind'. I also recall that when we were off duty during the week, two or three of us would go off dressed in 'civvies', hitch lifts to the West End and sign on for a day's casual work at Lyons Corner House. This involved making sandwiches for the cafeteria, serving coffee, even washing up, but it was of course flagrantly illegal and would have meant instant court martial if we had been caught. But the risk was always thought worth it when we got back to camp with several pounds to share out among our mates on a day when they didn't even have the price of a NAAFI 'wad' [bun] between them! This was the extent to which the shared comradeship of those days could be stretched. When we had nothing we had nothing together, and when we were 'flush' we all enjoyed it and celebrated together".

In January 1949 Fighter Command took over the operational control of the RAuxAF from Reserve Command, a sensible move in view of the modernisation of the RAuxAF fighter squadrons, which were then beginning conversion to jet aircraft. Administrative control was acquired on 1 November 1949.

A new AOC-in-C, AVM (acting AM) Sir Basil E. Embry KBE CB DSO DFC AFC, took over from AM Sir William Elliott on 19 April 1949. That year's major air exercise was named 'Foil', and was devoted to the trial of radio counter-measures. Held from 25 June to 3 July, the exercise involved Control & Reporting Units, the 11 and 12 Group Operations Rooms, and several GCI Stations, to which the staffs of GCI Stations outside the exercise area were posted for the duration of the exercise. Acting as observers, twenty-eight USAF and US Navy officers worked at Bentley Priory, and valuable lessons were learned.

Nine years after the Battle of Britain, a reunion dinner attended by eighty people

FIFTY YEARS OF PEACE

was held at the Priory on 15 September 1949, with Lord Dowding as guest of honour and Sir Basil Embry in the chair. The formation of a Battle of Britain Club was discussed at the dinner. For that year's Battle of Britain Day, Fighter Command provided both a marching party and a lining party at Westminster Abbey, with other personnel taking part in parades at Watford, Harrow and Radlett.

Extra personnel were posted to Bentley Priory in October 1949 to staff a Bulk Distribution Centre which was formed there to receive and distribute furniture, gardening equipment and anti-kerosene clothing.

During March 1950 the Royal Observer Corps was absorbed into Fighter Command, but the Corps retained its separate identity. From that time, ROC Groups were allocated to RAF sectors, so that a greater degree of coordination between the two could be created and maintained. At about the same time, the AOC-in-C Fighter Command decided, in view of the increasing threat from behind the Iron Curtain, that the Operations Room should be re-opened, and a Wg. Cdr. Fighter Controller was appointed to plan and coordinate the task for completion in six months. A new combined filtering and plotting system was to be introduced into the C&R system, and the design of new plotting tables began.

The Fighter Command exhibition which had been in position for over four years was closed down in June 1950 to allow for refurbishment of the Operations Room. During that time, 5000 people had visited the exhibition, including a number of Royal personages. Some of the more important exhibits were re-housed in a room adjacent to the Intelligence section.

Rapid development of the civil airways

Sports Day was clearly a significant event at Bentley Priory in the late 1940s. Here Lady Embry is seen presenting prizes, probably in 1949. [J. W. Tarrant]

system — invisible corridors in the sky along which airliners fly at predetermined spacings — was by 1950 becoming important to Fighter Command, and so on 1 August a satellite GCI Station was opened at Heathrow Airport to monitor flights of fighter aircraft crossing the airways. Meanwhile, interest in Russian military activities was growing, prompted by the outbreak of the war in Korea, and coastal GCI Stations were even more alert than usual.

As labour troubles in the British ports were rife at the time, twenty officers and fifty other ranks were sent on 10 July 1950 to Hornchurch, from where they moved surplus equipment to North Weald in order to make space for storage of imported foodstuffs. This task was named Operation 'Homeland'.

On 17 November 1950, Bentley Priory was on top form for the visit of HRH Princess Elizabeth. After arriving with her entourage at 11.15, the Princess, who two and a half years later would be crowned as Queen, inspected a guard of honour consisting of three officers, four SNCOs and 84 other ranks selected from a larger number drawn from Fighter Command units including, of course, Bentley Priory itself. Escorted by Gp. Capt. J. A. Tester, Princess Elizabeth visited the Operations Room, and after lunch watched a flying display in which the aircraft taking part were controlled by a mobile GCI unit parked in the grounds, explanations of the technique being provided by Sqn. Ldr. Mundy. Also displaying was a solitary de Havilland Hornet F.3 twin-engined fighter, PX349 of 65 Sqn., based at Linton-on-Ouse in Yorkshire. Its Sergeant pilot, Jack Sherburn, recalls how he practiced for the event, using Waterbeach in Cambridgeshire as a temporary base, but flying from nearby Bovingdon on the day itself. Afterwards, he heard that his efforts had been very well received by the Royal guest.

At the end of January 1951 the strength of the Fighter Command HQ Unit was 863, comprising 197 RAF and four WRAF officers, 543 airmen and 119 WRAFs. During April these numbers were increased slightly when the Central School of Aircraft Recognition was opened, with Flt. Lt. R. M. Dye in command. However, students of the School, all potential instructors in the RAF, ATC or ROC, were obliged to live at Hendon as no accommodation was available at Bentley Priory. The CSAR went on to hold courses at many RAF Stations as well as at Bentley Priory, and provided technical help in the shooting of recognition films. Assistance was also given to newsreel companies such as Pathé, and the unit drafted the Joint Services Aircraft Recognition Instructors' Manual.

Plans were drawn up early in 1951 for modifications to be made to the underground operations block to accommodate future automatic equipment, but in July the AOC-in-C decided against proceeding with the project. Instead he asked Air Ministry to agree in principle to build a completely new block to house the

De Havilland Hornet PX396 of 64 Squadron
[via R Sturtivant]

FIFTY YEARS OF PEACE

Operations Room and Defensive Radio Warfare (DRW) elements, the existing block to continue in use by the GPO and for signals equipment, the traffic office, PBX etc.

During June and July 1951, a number of Class 'G' reservists, mainly telegraphists but some plotters, were called up to Bentley Priory for fourteen days' refresher training, though with what degree of enthusiasm these men drawn back from civilian life performed is not recorded.

Battle of Britain parades in which Bentley Priory personnel took part were held at Christ Church, Watford, on 9 September 1951 and at St. Peter's Church, Bushey Heath, a week later, the latter a substantial event attended by three officers, 110 airmen and 40 WRAFs. Remembrance Sunday in November was also celebrated at Bushey Heath, while twenty airmen travelled to Westminster Cathedral to take part. Before long another ceremonial parade was held, the funeral of HM King George VI on 15 February 1952, in which a detachment of Fighter Command HQ Unit personnel took part.

Exercise 'Pinnacle' was held from 27 September to 8 October 1951, and eleven RAFVR officers, an SNCO and 49 other ranks worked at Metropolitan Sector Fighter Plotting Centre at Hill House, which was fully operational for the event. A new arrival at Hill House that year was Sqn. Ldr. Diana McCall, who says *"I often wonder what the local residents must have thought when thirty airmen/airwomen marched up the hill each day and disappeared into what looked like a normal house, and then, some hours later, marched down the hill again — rather like the Grand Old Duke of York!"* Diana also recalls that there was a magnificent rose garden at the Priory. *"This was the pride and joy of our bachelor Principal Medical Officer, who I think used to count the blooms daily. However, we girls used to 'pinch' some roses under cover of darkness, secrete them in our bosoms and run like hell back to our quarters, which were known as the 'Casbah'!"*

Modernisation of air defences

As part of a general modernisation of the defences of the UK, a new unit - Air Defence Operations Centre (ADOC) - was formed at Bentley Priory on 23 February 1953. Although a separate organisation, ADOC was administered by Fighter Command HQ Unit, Stanmore Park. ADOC's role was to provide the facilities with which the Air Defence Commander could direct and coordinate the air defence operations of the UK. Its precise functions were to be aware of any immediate threat to the UK and to advise Sector operations rooms accordingly; to maintain an appropriate state of readiness throughout the UK air defences; to initiate or authorise inter-Sector air reinforcements as needed to counter any airborne threat; and to provide a technical intelligence network. In command of ADOC was its senior Controller, Gp. Capt. D. C. Stapleton CBE DFC AFC. Each month from February to October 1953 a synthetic air defence exercise was staged so that

Vampire F.3 VF335 [via R Sturtivant]

staff could be trained in wartime conditions, any extra personnel being provided by HQ Fighter Command and by reservists. A major exercise, code-named 'Momentum', was held in August, and ADOC staff were divided into five teams, each consisting of a controller, deputy controller, signals officer, intelligence officer and their staffs.

Another new Fighter Command unit, 80 Wing, came into being on 1 August 1953, with headquarters at Bentley Priory. It was formed to take over three Radio Countermeasures squadrons from 70 Wing, and functional control was to be exercised by ADOC. Three Signals Units, 253, 744 and 869 SUs, were transferred to 80 Wing from 90 Group. At first the Wing had no CO, but on 12 October Wg. Cdr. J. A. Vigor arrived to take up his duties. Fighter Command HQ was now charged with exercising command and control over all ground radio warfare facilities operating in support of all Commands in an air war. 80 Wing was required to operate, maintain and control monitoring, jamming, 'spoof' systems and decoy lighting systems, and to do so contained Operations, Technical, Administrative and Equipment branches.

ADOC became fully operational in October 1953 and was then normally manned for six and a half hours each day except during exercises, when full manning was in force. On 9 November, Gp. Capt. Stapleton was replaced by Gp. Capt. J. H. Lapsley OBE AFC, who oversaw Exercise 'Magna Flux' between 1 and 6 March 1954. This exercise, designed to test the effectiveness of the penetrating techniques of a modern jet bomber force against an alert air defence system, was considered to have been highly successful, with continuity of tracking by the Control & Reporting System particularly efficient. 'Magna Flux' was also the first major exercise for the new 80 Wing. Shortly afterwards came 'Prune Two', in which 80 Wing co-ordinated the radio countermeasures effort. The Signals Units under 80 Wing control made deployments to UK locations from time to time to monitor radio security.

During Exercise 'Dividend', held from 16 to 25 July 1954, the ADOC plotters were supplemented by 153 members of 7204 Reserve Flt., based at Stanmore Park, who arrived at Bentley Priory on 10 July for refresher training, as did five SNCOs, 29 fighter plotters and nineteen radar operators from 2nd TAF in Germany. From the Control & Reporting school at RAF Middle Wallop came 64 fighter plotters. All these extra 'bods' were accommodated at Stanmore Park.

A good deal of reconstruction and refurbishment was carried out at Bentley Priory in the early 1950s in order to maintain the fabric of this highly valuable building. Above the rebuilt ante-room a new conference room was formed on the second floor in 1953, while in 1954 external restoration began and the Officers' Mess kitchen and servery were modernised and enlarged. Completing this phase of work, the dining room was re-roofed and extended in 1955. 80 Wing staff moved into their new office block in May 1955, work having begun a year earlier.

Wg. Cdr. E. C. Sealey MBE took over as CO of 80 Wing on 20 August 1956 but a month later was posted to Air Ministry and was succeeded by Sqn. Ldr. D. G. Salter, who had been the Wing's senior operations officer since its formation.

On 1 September 1956 the Movement Liaison Section of the Centralised Filter Plotting Centre, formerly based at Hill House, moved to Bentley Priory so that Hill House could be de-requisitioned. The task of this small unit, which received the flight plans of military and civilian aircraft from Uxbridge ATCC and Heathrow Airport, was to pass the information by telephone to airfields which needed to have it. Upon arrival at Bentley Priory, the MLS was retitled Metropolitan Raid Recognition Centre (MRRC), an apparently inappropriate title. For the first two weeks, a severe shortage of telephone lines caused outbound movements to be disregarded. Exercise 'Stronghold', held at this time, showed how easily the system could be saturated. Twenty-four hour manning

FIFTY YEARS OF PEACE

RAF BENTLEY PRIORY
UNDERGROUND OPERATIONS BLOCK
Sketch plan as at September 1954.

Upper Level

Key
1 - W/C.
2 - NCO i/c PBX.
3 - PBX Rest Room.
4 - Controller's Dais.
5 - Controller's Dais.
6 - Control Cabin.
7 - Tactical Intelligence Cabin.
8 - Operations B.
9 - Laison Balcony.
10 - Directing Staff Cabin.
11 - Tote Operator.
12 - Teleprinters.
13 - Tube Exchange.
14 - Ops. PBX
15 - GPO racking
16 - AOC-in-C's Conference Room
17 - PBX
18 - WO i/c Ops.
19 - NCO i/c trg.
20 - Stairs
21 - Kitchen
22 - Cleaners Cupboard.
23 - Emergency Lighting Battery Room
24 - DRW Room
25 - GPO Workshop
26 - Supervisors Dais
27 - Supervisor
28 - Computer Room
29 - GPO Workshop
30 - Ops. Store
31 - Battery Room

97

began on 1 November, although the staffing situation did not allow for absence on leave. There were four officers, four NCOs and forty other ranks, one of whom was 2760315 LAC Burgess D. C., a National Serviceman who represented Great Britain in the Olympic Games at Melbourne. The staff situation became even worse, only 21 other ranks being available for duty at the end of January 1957. Meanwhile, 80 Wing's task was now regarded by the Air Ministry as completed, and on 15 March 1957 the Wing disbanded.

On 1 April 1957 MRRC was retitled again, this time becoming Metropolitan Air Defence Notification Centre (MADNC). During that summer great interest was aroused by the tracking of 'Zombie' flights — Russian airliners using Heathrow Airport. Yet another change of title came about on 1 December 1957, when, following the closure of Southern ADNC at Rudloe Manor, operational responsibility was transferred to MADNC, which now became known as ADNC (South). The unit's establishment of personnel increased, although no more airmen arrived to fill the vacancies! Extra land-lines were installed from the radar stations at Ventnor and Sopley and from ATCC Gloucester. Three months later ADNC (South) assumed the operational responsibility of ADNC (East) and twelve airmen were posted in. New connections were made with radars at Neatishead, Trimingham and Wartling and with the ATCC at Watnall. At the same time Beachy Head and St. Margarets ceased to function as reporting stations. Very soon, political tension in the Middle East caused twenty-four hour manning to become a regular feature of ADNC (South).

The 40th anniversary of the formation of the Royal Air Force was celebrated in April 1958 by a presentation to members of the Royal family. Music was provided by pipe bands from Kinloss and Halton. Great trouble had been taken in the selection of 76 NCOs, other ranks and civilians to undertake duties as waiters, barmen and cloakroom attendants, and all had to be security-cleared and specially kitted-out. They were all accommodated at Stanmore Park for four days, which included a period of training for the event. Sqn. Ldr. Diana McCall recalls that she was one of only three WRAF officers who attended, the others being Sqn.. Ldr. Paine and the Matron of RAF Hospital Uxbridge. *"A hundred officers gathered in the Rotunda at 22.00 hours. I talked to the Duke of Edinburgh and Princess Marina, Duchess of Kent "* she says. *"At the briefing before the reception Gp. Capt. Foxley-Norris had told us not to 'gawp' at royalty, but this proved impossible as the entire Royal family was present "*.

Visitors, as always, were well received

The colourful chevron markings on the fuselage and crest on the tail indicate that WS665 was a Meteor NF12 belonged to 153 Squadron of Fighter Command. [G. Cruikshank]

at Bentley Priory, and in 1958 included on 6 February the Turkish Air Attaché (Col. Mustapha Azakli); on 22 April the C-in-C of the Royal Norwegian Air Force (Lt. Gen. Motzfeldt); and next day the VCAS Netherlands Air Force (Maj. Gen. Zielstra) arrived. All were no doubt keen to see the latest developments in the air defence business. From May, the ADNC(S) staff maintained a 24-hour watch system and frequent exercises were held.

By the late 1950s it was becoming clear that the Air Defence Commander, working in ADOC at Bentley Priory, needed information on nuclear fallout and bomb-bursts in order to deploy fighter aircraft effectively. It was decided that the ROC, whose aircraft-plotting function was now becoming very difficult due to the high speeds and altitudes involved, would become responsible for monitoring information on nuclear activity, although still maintaining a watch on low-altitude aircraft. During the spring of 1958 officers of the ROC visited ADOC, where in a synthetic exercise the plotting table was used to build up a picture of nuclear fallout. From that time, frequent exercises were held to perfect the fallout function, and a programme of construction of underground posts to replace the wartime-vintage structures was started. Unfortunately, many ROC members considered the new job uninteresting and left the Corps.

Planning for a reorganised air defence system to come into use in 1962-64 began at Fighter Command in June 1958. New radars were envisaged, with automatic data handling and the use of computers, and it was considered that fighter aircraft would be controlled from not more than two centres.

New equipment installed at Bentley Priory for the benefit of ADNC (South) in September 1958 was an early type of facsimile machine. Known as Mufax, it was put into use for a two-week trial period in which flight plans could be sent to Bawdsey in the form of a route map, and it was found that sending such a document took 4 minutes 45 seconds. However, at the end of the Mufax trial period, ADNC (South) disbanded. From 1 October 1958, an Air Defence Notification Centre became operational at each ATCC — Uxbridge, Gloucester, Watnall, Preston and Prestwick.

In the late 1950s, an extensive enquiry was carried out by an Air Ministry working party headed by AM Sir Hubert Patch into United Kingdom airspace and air traffic problems. The project was completed early in 1959, and on 23 February the Air Council approved the working party's recommendation that an independent authority should be set up to deal with such problems. The proposed authority would represent the three British armed services, the USAF and the Ministry of Supply (later the Ministry of Aviation). Initially, a nucleus known as Air

Checkerboard marks either side of the fuselage roundel show that Hawker Hunter fighter XE647 was from 63 Sqn.
[G. Cruikshank]

RAF BENTLEY PRIORY AND STANMORE PARK

Traffic Services Headquarters (ATSHQ) would be established, comprising existing staff of the UK Air Traffic Branch of Fighter Command HQ and the Air Traffic Control Special Projects Section at RAF Shawbury.

On 26 February 1959 Fighter Command HQ received five photographs purporting to show a UFO hovering at a height of about 200 feet (133m.) above the runway at Heathrow Airport the previous day! Having studied the pictures, staff at Bentley Priory sent them on to the Air Ministry, the response of which was that it was thought that no significance should be attached to them!

ATSHQ duly formed in building 82 at Bentley Priory on 18 June 1959, under the command of Gp. Capt. F. J. Robinson OBE DFC. Its main remit was to act as co-ordinating authority on the use of UK airspace by military aircraft in the safest and most efficient manner. In addition, ATSHQ took over the running of the five ATCCs and the three ATC radar units, Sopley, Heathrow and Hack Green. A third task was to cooperate with the Ministry of Transport & Civil Aviation on policy matters affecting military and civilian aircraft. A range of subsidiary projects included the preparation of a specification for a joint civil/military ATCC in the southern region, a study of East Anglia's special air traffic problems and a merger between the Gloucester and Uxbridge ATCCs.

With all these tasks to carry out, ATSHQ left Bentley Priory on 14 September 1959 to move the short distance to *'Kestrel Grove'*, with a minor change of title to United Kingdom Air Traffic Services (UKATS). In command from 28 September was Air Cdre. H. J. Hickey CBE. On 1 February 1960 UKATS took over operational control of the ADNCs from Fighter Command HQ. A further change of title came about on 1 January 1961, when UKATS became HQ Military Air Traffic Operations (HQMATO).

Routine exercises occupied ADOC personnel during the next few years, with little to mark the passing of time. Interludes took place in August 1961, when on two occasions a BBC TV film unit

A dramatic picture of English Electric Lightning F.6 XR724 about to depart. Nine Fighter Command/Strike Command Squadrons flew Lightnings from 1960.
[J. Betts]

FIFTY YEARS OF PEACE

Gloster Javelin FAW9 night-fighter XH888 'K' of 23 Squadron. [Author]

shot scenes at Bentley Priory, and in September when an Air Ministry documentary film was made there by Verity Films. At the time, ADOC's strength was 172 personnel.

Reconstruction of the ADOC operations room was completed in August 1962, after which Exercise 'Fallex 62' was held to synthetically test the complete NATO offensive and defensive capability. It was during this exercise that, on 21 September 1962 at 02.15 hours GMT, ADOC was 'destroyed' by an imaginary 10-megaton weapon!

An important development took place on 1 October 1962, when ADOC, by now recovered from its synthetic destruction, took over from Patrington GCI Station the responsibility for Quick Reaction Alert (QRA) aircraft and missiles. Tracks of Russian 'Bear' long-range patrol aircraft flying at up to 35,000 feet off western Scotland were fed to ADOC on 22 November, the first time these aircraft had operated in that area. On 18 February 1964, by which time the BMEWS facility at Fylingdales had become operational, a 'Bear' being tracked by the radar station at Saxa Vord flew within a mile of that Station and later close to another station on the Faeroes. The aircraft, thought to be on a radar-interrogation mission, then turned north-east and flew back to Russia via northern Norway. This was the first Russian aircraft known to have approached British airspace.

Problems diagnosed in the Priory
A surveyor reported in 1964 that the ante-room in the Priory, which had been rebuilt in 1947 after the fire, was affected by dry rot, even though steel beams had been used in the rebuilding. All work on the building stopped at once pending a more comprehensive report, but it was to be several years before the full extent of the problem was realised. In the operations block, work on the air-conditioning system in December 1964 revealed that the main wall of the ADOC plant room was dangerously cracked, but after emergency jacks had been placed in position it was found that the wall was not load-bearing. Although the contractors are said to have shown little or no interest in meeting their contract completion date, by May 1965 the control 'bridge' was re-occupied.

MATO, meanwhile, had been working on its allotted tasks for some years, but on 1 February 1965 completed a move from *'Kestrel Grove'* to Hillingdon House at Uxbridge. At the same time it was proposed that a joint ROC/Home Office headquarters should be set up at *'Kestrel Grove'*, but as this building was to be de-requisitioned nothing came of this idea. ROC HQ then moved into Bentley Priory.

Synthetic exercises continued, and on 5 December 1965 X-Raid 116 (the 116th plot of a Russian aircraft near UK airspace) was logged by ADOC. This time it was two 'Bears' which were intercepted and 'seen off' by USAF fighters based on Iceland, but

RAF BENTLEY PRIORY AND STANMORE PARK

McDonnell Douglas Phamton XT900 streams its braking parachute at RAF Coningsby. [Simon Peters]

seven more such incidents occurred later in the month. Much more interesting to many was the sighting of four unidentified flying objects on 16 December. Reported to Bentley Priory by local civilians at 19.25 hours, the UFOs flew across the sky from south-east to north-west showing bright green lights, trailing sparks and each spinning on its axis. A similar report came in five minutes later from a witness at Edmonton.

Her Majesty the Queen paid a visit to review the Royal Observer Corps on 24 June 1966, and presented the ROC standard to Observer Officer John Ballington. Greeted by the Lord Lieutenant of Greater London, Field Marshal Earl Alexander of Tunis, Her Majesty was also welcomed by the Mayor, Cllr. E. G. Buckle and the Mayoress. Taking part in the parade were 706 members of the ROC, among them Chief Observer T. E. Bee, who told the Queen that he had joined in 1925, when the Observer Corps was formed!

Strike Command

In 1968 a reorganisation of the Command structure of the RAF took place, included in which was the merger on 30 April of Fighter Command and Bomber Command to form a new body, Strike Command. Such a far-reaching move could not be allowed to pass without a suitable ceremony, particularly in view of the magnificent work done by both Commands over their thirty-odd years of existence in peace and war. At Bentley Priory, therefore, a parade was held at the end of April, during which the AOC-in-C Fighter Command, AM Sir Frederick Rosier CB CBE DSO, inspected those taking part, and twenty-four Lightnings, four Hunters, three Meteors and a single Canberra flew overhead. Several ace fighter pilots of the Second World War were present, including AVM J. E. 'Johnny' Johnson, Gp. Capt. Peter Townsend, Wg. Cdr. R. 'Bob' Stanford Tuck, Air Cdre. A. C. 'Al' Deere, Gp. Capt. Douglas Bader and Air Cdre P. M. 'Pete' Brothers.

With the disbandment of Fighter Command, Bentley Priory lost some of its status, but there was still plenty of work to be done! On the day of the merger Bentley Priory became the headquarters of 11 (Fighter) Group of Strike Command, the first AOC-in-C of which was ACM Sir Wallace Kyle GCB CBE DSO DFC. In addition to the staff of the new 11 Group, who used an office block close to the eastern end of the Priory building, administrative staff of Strike Command HQ took up residence at Bentley Priory in two large office blocks which had been built in 1959-61. The AOC 11 Group, his SASO and staff occupied the offices in the Priory itself. They would have witnessed the filming in 1969 of the closing sequence for the film 'Battle of Britain', in a most fitting location.

A break with the past took place on 1 March 1971, when the Air Defence Operations Centre left to be incorporated into the Strike Command Operations Centre at RAF High Wycombe, where on completion of new buildings it was joined early in 1973 by the Strike Command HQ

FIFTY YEARS OF PEACE

Tornado 'DK' on display in a hangar. Several Tornado squadrons were administered by 11 Group at Bentley Priory.
[Simon Peters]

staff. This move allowed the AOC 11 Group and his staff to move out of the Priory building and into the upper floor of the recently-vacated eastern office block in June 1974. Another unit which now came to the end of its useful life was the Control & Reporting Evaluation Team, which disbanded on 28 February 1973. The underground bunker was, however, retained in serviceable condition for use as a standby should the High Wycombe bunker be put out of action.

During 1974 a comprehensive survey of the Priory building costing £35,000 revealed that dry rot had spread and had a hold on the building. The Department of the Environment declared the main part of the building, apart from the dining room and kitchen area, unsafe for anything other than normal day-to-day use, and that the main part of the building would have to be closed in March 1975. This decision caused a major problem to the Royal Air Forces Association, which was in the advanced stage of planning a Fighter Command Commemoration Ball at Bentley Priory to be held in July 1974. To overcome the problem, large marquees were erected in the grounds and the lower floor of the Priory was strengthened temporarily, allowing a very successful Ball to be held.

Prominent at this event was the Queen Mother, who showed great interest in the future of the Priory, and soon a campaign to save the building began. There remained the problem of providing alternative public accommodation, and in the very difficult economic situation only £10,000 was available to convert the office block vacated earlier by Strike Command HQ staff, although £9,000 more was found later.

On 4 November 1977 it was announced that a million-pound redevelopment scheme would take place, for completion in 1981. The Officers & Aircrew Selection Centre would then move to Bentley Priory from Biggin Hill, while Stanmore Park would close except for the married quarters there. However, eventually it was decided that major expansion was not compatible with the residential nature of the district, and these proposals were not activated. Not to be forgotten, however, Bentley Priory was used in 1975 by Thames TV for scenes in some episodes of the popular *'Get Some In!'* series set in a fictional School of Recruit Training.

The Great Fire

Even though major expansion at Bentley Priory had been ruled out, it was decided in 1978 that the main building should be refurbished at a cost of about £1 million to provide a larger Officers' Mess. After most of the collection of valuable paintings and other artefacts had been taken to the MU at Quedgeley for safety, the contractors, Cubitts, began work, using a spirit-based wood preservative on the roof timbers of the Priory building. During the evening of 21 June 1979 smoke was seen issuing from the building, and within minutes fire had taken hold of the Priory. The fire brigade arrived quickly and several firemen ventured inside, managing to get the fire under control, but the electricity supply had not been turned off, and firemen who approached the seat of the blaze found themselves in the midst of showers of sparks and had to retreat. By the time the electricity had been cut off the fire had spread. When three men were injured in an attempt to regain control it was decided that the building was too dangerous to re-enter and the fire was allowed to burn itself out. In the cold light of day it was established that the fire was caused accidentally by either a cigarette end left smouldering or by an electric light being left on, either factor igniting the highly volatile wood preservative. The main staircase was destroyed, but the fire missed the Adelaide Room and destroyed the rooms on either side. Insurance covered rebuilding, and on 21 August 1979 the Local Authority approved previously-rejected plans to erect new buildings at Bentley Priory totalling an area reduced from 201,000 sq.ft. (18,680 sq.m.) to 182,000 sq.ft. (16,914 sq.m.). At an eventual cost of £3.1 million, work was completed early in 1982 and the pictures and other relics restored to their former glory. It seems possible that had the fire not happened such large-scale work might not have been carried out! Subsequently, plaques measuring 3.5" x 4.5" (89mm. x 114mm.) were made bearing the Fighter Command crest and a plate reading 'Part of the oak flooring of Bentley Priory, Headquarters Fighter Command, from where Air Chief Marshal Lord Dowding directed the Battle of Britain'. These were sold for £5.00 each. After completion of the work, Bentley Priory was officially re-

Hurricane Mk.II LF751, painted in the markings of 24 Operational Training Unit, with which it served during the war years, stands guard while a fire engine crew make sure that the 1979 fire at Bentley Priory has been extinguished. [Harrow local history collection]

FIFTY YEARS OF PEACE

opened by Her Majesty the Queen on 24 June 1982. More construction work took place in 1983/84, when the underground operations room was greatly extended.

One of Bentley Priory's current units, the Systems Development Centre, was formed on 1 April 1983, and was joined on 1 September 1984 by the RAF Regiment Training Evaluation Staff, who moved in from RAF Catterick. To merge into the Systems Development Centre, the computer software experts of UK Air Defence Ground Environment (UKADGE) arrived from RAF Wattisham on 25 September 1985. By January 1986 11 Group's title had been modified to 11 (Air Defence) Group in deference to the Group's revised function. The RAF Regt. staff who had arrived in 1984 left again on 30 March 1990 to move to RAF North Luffenham.

At the end of July 1991 Her Majesty the Queen and Prince Phillip visited Bentley Priory to participate in the de-activation of the Royal Observer Corps and

Bentley Priory seen from the air soon after the disastrous fire in 1979. The temporary roof cover under which the contractors were working at the time is clearly visible.[Crown copyright]

RAF BENTLEY PRIORY AND STANMORE PARK

A fireman gazes on the scene of devastation at the foot of the main staircase at Bentley Priory just after the fire in June 1979. [Crown Copyright via RAF Bentley Priory]

coincidentally the 50th anniversary of the use of the word 'Royal' in the title. Two thousand members of the ROC were present, and the aircraft of the Battle of Britain Memorial Flight flew past. Senior Administrative Officer of the ROC at the time was Mr. N. A. Greig MBE, who then became known as the Senior ROC Officer, remaining in this post until the final disbandment of the ROC.

So ended fifty years of peacetime work at RAF Bentley Priory, years which had seen some intense activity during the dark days of the 'Cold War', when the security of the free world had been threatened again, balanced by many years of routine defence tasks. Now, the dissolution of the USSR followed the October 1990 merger of East and West Germany into a new state, these events having a relaxing effect on the defences of all NATO countries. There had also been some involvement of 11 Group personnel in the Gulf War. The second fifty years thus began on a more peaceful note, and personnel at the Priory devoted themselves to well-proven routines, though of course ever vigilant.

In spite of the fire, ACM Sir Hugh Dowding's office at Bentley Priory has been preserved in its original condition, with the original furniture and fittings. [author]

RAF BENTLEY PRIORY AND STANMORE PARK

Chapter 5

RAF Bentley Priory Today

RAF Bentley Priory today is, in terms of numbers of personnel, a shadow of its former self, but remains a vital element in the defence of the United Kingdom. As part of the overall scheme, authority was given for the formation of the Sector Operations Centre UK (SOCUK) on 1 April 1995, a unit tasked with maintaining overall command and control of UK air defence.

11 (Air Defence) Group merged on 1 April 1996 with 18 Group to form 11/18 Group, although 18 Group's assets and personnel remained at Fleet Headquarters, Northwood. A ceremony was staged at Bentley Priory to mark the occasion, with officers and men of 16 Sqn., RAF Regiment, based at RAF Honington in Suffolk, providing the guard of honour. Standards of 5, 8, 11, 22, 25, 29, 42(R), 43, 51, 56(R), 100, 111, 120, 201, 202 and 206 Squadrons, with escorts, formed the main part of the parade, at which the salute was taken by the new Group's AOC, AVM Cliff Spink CBE. Present for the ceremony were a number of former 11 and 18 Group AOCs. The combined Group is responsible for air defence, maritime operations, electronic warfare and search-and-rescue activities over the whole of the United Kingdom. Coinciding with the merger, SOCUK transferred to High Wycombe.

Later in the year the Inspectorate of Flight Safety (IFS) moved to Bentley Priory from Adastral House in central London and took up residence in the former Royal Observer Corps offices. The present Inspector, Air Cdre. R. Peacock-Edwards, decided to mark the move from London by inviting as many former Inspectors as possible, together with representatives of British Airways, the

A nice picture taken in November 1981, of Bentley Priory with one of its 'guardian' aircraft, Spitfire Mk.XVI SL574, in the markings of 234 Squadron (although that unit never flew Spitfires of that Mark!). [Crown copyright]

RAF BENTLEY PRIORY AND STANMORE PARK

Bentley Priory seen from the Italian garden on the south side in 1981. [Harrow local history collection]

Civil Aviation Authority and the Air Accident Investigation Branch of the Department of Transport.

In March 1997 Lord Dowding of Bentley Priory was once again in the public eye, when his medals were purchased by the RAF Museum for the world record sum of £69,000. Although the collection had been scheduled for auction, a sale was negotiated with the auctioneers after an approach by the museum on behalf of Odette, Baroness Dowding, the widow of ACM Dowding's only son. The intention is that the medals will be on display in the RAF Museum's Battle of Britain Hall, alongside the surviving medals of Reichsmarshal Goering, Dowding's adversary in 1940.

Still at readiness!

At Bentley Priory, the underground operations block, to which further small extensions were made in 1995, is maintained in an operational condition for use at 60 minutes' notice should a national emergency develop. If that happened, four operators drafted in from Strike Command at High Wycombe would oversee the entire UK defence situation. Modern radar screens and high-powered computers take up far less space than the large plotting tables of former years, but the current

The entrance hall at Bentley Priory typifies the high quality of the building and its furnishings. [author]

RAF BENTLEY TODAY

The Officers' Mess anteroom in the Priory building, showing some of the aviation paintings which hang on the walls.[author]

Personnel of the Air Warfare Centre at Bentley Priory study and develop operational doctrines and conduct battle management training. At times several of the students are middle-ranking officers of other NATO air forces. More obvious from its title is the task of the Inspectorate of Flight Safety, which runs courses for flight safety officers, flying authorisers and NATO flying supervisors. Accommodation for the IFS includes a purpose-built theatre, named the Hayr Lecture Theatre after the first Inspector of Flight Safety, AM Sir Kenneth Hayr.

system is clearly much more efficient. Above ground, the Systems Development Centre, the RAF Inspectorate of Flight Safety, an element of the Air Warfare Centre and the headquarters of 11/18 Group all contribute to one aim — the defence of these islands.

A joint military and civilian unit, the Systems Development Centre is responsible for general software support, computer systems testing and fault analysis on behalf of IUKADGE — the Improved United Kingdom Air Defence Ground Environment. Many of the computer programmers are civilians, and their work on the ICCS (Integrated Computer Control System) forms the core task of the SDC. The unit is responsible for 'configuration management' — ensuring that all IUKADGE elements are using exactly the same software.

Bentley Priory is maintained in first-class condition, as befits such a historic building. Many portraits of prominent Battle of Britain pilots such as Douglas Bader, Johnny Johnson and Al Deere hang on the walls of its public rooms, while on the inner wall of the 'porte cochére' and

An ornate staircase which climbs from the Bentley Priory entrance hall to a columned landing. [author]

109

RAF BENTLEY PRIORY AND STANMORE PARK

In the grounds of RAF Bentley Priory stands a symbol of post-war Fighter Command in the form of Lightning F.1a XM173 (8414M), painted in the colours of 56 Squadron, with which it served in the early 1960s. It continued to fly with other units until being struck off charge in 1974 at RAF Binbrook. The missile attached to the fuselage is a dummy! [author]

protected from the elements are mounted a number of nameplates retrieved from scrapped 'Battle of Britain' class steam locomotives. Within the dining room and corridor can be seen a selection of aviation paintings by prominent artists. Air Marshal Dowding's office, looking out onto the Italian garden, is maintained as a small museum, with combat reports signed by fighter pilots, photograph albums and squadron badges on display, as well as the desk and other furniture and equipment used by Dowding during the Battle of Britain. A large wall display shows the Order of Battle for 18 August 1940. The ladies' room, used as the filter room from 1936 to 1940, and the ante room, the temporary operations room during the same period, have been restored to their former condition.

To look after its administration, RAF Bentley Priory has a Station Commander, at the time of writing Sqn. Ldr. Geraldine Wilson. To compensate for the closure of RAF Stanmore Park, a sergeants' mess and living accommodation for airmen are to be built at Bentley Priory by the end of 1998, in view of which there seems to be reason to hope that the Priory will continue in use well past the Millennium, with the 75th anniversary of RAF ownership being marked on 1 June 2001.

A fine aerial view of RAF Bentley Priory in recent years. The main Priory building with its prominent clocktower is seen at centre, with the post-war office block now used by HQ 11/18 Group to the right and the Systems Development Centre behind that. The underground bunker is on the extreme right of the picture, while on the left are seen more of the modern office blocks which house support staff. In front of the Priory is the south-facing Italian garden, separated from the parkland by a retaining wall. [RAF Bentley Priory]

Chapter 6

Stanmore Park: The War Years

To the dismay of many residents of the quiet town of Stanmore, the Air Ministry acquired the Stanmore Park mansion and estate in 1938. Contractors promptly set about demolishing the property, using traction engines hauling wire ropes, and grubbed out many fine old trees, including rare willow-leaved oaks. Harrow Urban District Council, fore-runner of the present London Borough of Harrow, was not consulted about the work, which was regarded by many as an act of high-handed official vandalism, especially as a good deal of money had been spent by the Council in improving local amenities and the environment generally. Nevertheless, construction of a hutted camp for use by the Royal Air Force went quickly ahead in those days of heightened anxiety about a possible conflict, and in December 1938 RAF Stanmore Park came into existence as a base for balloons which would form part of the London barrage. The camp was bounded by Uxbridge Road on the north, Old Church Lane on the east and The Chase to the west, and included in the property was Temple Pond, on the south side near Gordon Avenue. Very prominent, and regarded as an eyesore by local residents, were two hangars, both 70 feet (21.3m.) high, which stood close to the Uxbridge Road boundary of the Station. Also provided from an early date were winch and trailer sheds for use by balloon-operating personnel.

Arrival of the 'Blimps'

As soon as the Station was open, two balloon squadrons, 906 and 907 Sqns., were activated at RAF Stanmore Park as units of the Auxiliary Air Force (AuxAF), and the attestation of recruits, all part-time voluntary men, began. Each squadron comprised five Flights, with nine balloons to a Flight. 907 Sqn. even managed to find time to appoint the Rt. Hon. Earl of Athlone as Honorary Air Commodore before the end of the year.

To administer the two squadrons, 3 Balloon Centre came into being in January 1939. The Centre's first CO was Wg. Cdr. E. A. Bald MC, who took up the appointment on 14 March and who, as Gp. Capt. Bald, was the first Station

How history is often recorded - a tiny snapshot in someone's photo-album of Stanmore Park house on 6 February 1938, just before the building was demolished to make way for the RAF Station.
[Harrow local history collection]

RAF BENTLEY PRIORY AND STANMORE PARK

In Old Church Lane, Stanmore, stood 'The Manor House', a mock Tudor edifice used as Headquarters Balloon Command from September 1939 to February 1940, then Headquarters Air Training Corps, and finally as the home of the AOC-in-C Fighter Command from July 1954. [Harrow local history collection]

Commander, from 13 September 1939. Recruitment to the two squadrons proceeded amid a growing realisation that war with Germany was inevitable. One of the recruiting methods used was to take balloons out for public inspection at sites such as the Empire State Cinema at Kilburn and the Ambassador Theatre at Hendon, which were visited by 906 Sqn. in February 1939. The final Empire Air Day at Halton was another venue where it was hoped recruits might be gained.

During the first half of 1939, recruitment continued, building the two squadrons up to full strength. On 11 June, a quarter of the personnel of each squadron were embodied (called up for temporary full-time service), each man serving on a balloon site for three days before returning to Stanmore for further training. A second period of embodiment began, with different personnel, on 7 July, each squadron providing a few officers and about 160 other ranks, and a third period on 6 August, by which time the international situation was deteriorating rapidly.

Preparations for war
Call-up notices were sent to all personnel on 23 August 1939, and full mobilisation took place next day. On 1 September, among those called to Stanmore Park were the members of 13 (RAF) Coy. of the ATS, one of 47 such units formed before the Women's Auxiliary Air Force became effective, although it had been created as a separate service by Royal Warrant on 28 July 1939. Within twenty-four hours, both squadrons had been deployed to war sites, each with balloons inflated and flown. While this was taking place, 907 Squadron's headquarters left Stanmore Park and moved to Harringay greyhound stadium. By 1 September the balloon barrage around London was fully active, the 'blimps' flying at their maximum 4500 ft. (1370m.) altitude.

The balloon goes up!
After being formed on 1 November 1938 at Kelvin House, Cleveland St., London W1, HQ Balloon Command moved on 1 September 1939, two days before the outbreak of war, to *'Manor House'* in Old Church Lane, Stanmore, using some of 3 Balloon Centre's premises at Stanmore Park as living accommodation. In command as AOC-in-C was AVM O. T. Boyd CB OBE MC AFC. By the outbreak of war, Balloon Command had been divided into four Groups, numbered 30 to 33. With an establishment of 450 balloons, 30 Group controlled 1 to 4 Balloon Centres in the

STANMORE PARK: THE WAR YEARS

A group fo WAAF's learn about the intricacies of Barrage Balloon rigging on a model.

London area, which in turn administered 901 to 910 Squadrons; 31 Group, with 499 balloons, looked after 5 to 10 Balloon Centres in the Midlands, which administered 911 to 926 and 929 Squadrons; 32 Group, the smallest, had 200 balloons in the south of England and Wales and controlled 11 to 14 Balloon Centres and 927, 928, 930 to 935 Squadrons; and finally 33 Group, with 368 balloons in the north of England and in Scotland, looked after 15 to 19 Balloon Centres and 936 to 949 Squadrons. Included in the organisation was 3 Balloon Centre at Stanmore, which controlled 906 and 907 Sqns. To maintain this considerable force, new balloons were being delivered at the rate of 250 per month at the beginning of 1940, while 500 balloons per month were being repaired.

Previously known as *'The Croft'*, *'Manor House'*, built in 1901, had been bought in 1928 by Mr. Samuel Wallrock, who wanted its 4.5 acre (1.8 hectare) grounds on which to build himself a substantial home. He employed local builder Douglas Wood to convert his dreams into reality. First a mock-Tudor gatehouse was erected, followed by a similar garage and a building known as *'Church House'*, in which old building materials were used to make a baronial-style banqueting hall. So pleasing to Mr. Wallrock were the results of his builder's efforts that he decided to completely remodel *'Manor House'* along the same lines, and a great deal of money, effort and attention to detail went into the project. Similar efforts were put into the gardens, in which mature trees from several parts of the world were planted. It seems, however, that Mr. Wallrock over-reached himself financially, as in 1933 he was declared bankrupt and left the property, which remained empty and neglected until the RAF took over.

At *'Manor House'*, personnel were at first accommodated in the banqueting hall. Next day, work began digging trenches for the protection of staff, and *'Yew Tree Cottage'* in Old Church Lane was taken over as the officers' mess. Other properties in the same road were requisitioned — *'Friars Mead'* for signals personnel, *'Cherry Tree'* and *'The Beeches'*. The AOC-in-C Balloon Command took up residence in the main building with his SASO and signals officers.

RAF BENTLEY PRIORY AND STANMORE PARK

Ground crews start to 'walk' a barrage baloon out of its storage hangar.

Air Ministry had ordered, during the morning of 1 September, that balloons were to be inflated and flown at a height not exceeding 100 feet (30m.), and in all 450 balloons were flying over London that day and 203 in the provinces. Early in the morning of 3 September HQ Balloon Command instructed all Groups under its control to fly balloons at altitude to counter any possible German attack, although this was over eight hours before Neville Chamberlain made his famous speech.

For defence and security duties, 'E' Coy., 2nd. Bn. Princess Louise's Regt., comprising three officers, 9 NCOs and 105 other ranks, arrived on 8 September to relieve 'H' Coy. of the same Regiment, which had been in place since 29 August. One of their first tasks was in connection with a signal sent from Air Ministry on 9 September warning recipients about a black saloon car, the occupant of which, dressed as an RAF officer, had been seen loitering in various places. 'H' Coy. returned on 26 September, however.

Each of the balloons available at the time had its own lorry carrying a winch and towing a trailer loaded with hydrogen cylinders. A crew of ten manned each balloon, which travelled as a complete unit to its own site. The function of the balloon barrage was to defeat low raids, discourage attacks on large cities and create the impression in the minds of enemy pilots that the barrage was much bigger than it really was! When operational, Balloon Groups notified Fighter Command HQ whether balloons were flying ('shining') or close-hauled ('dull').

Problems experienced by balloon crews in those early days included the effects of gales or lightning, which destroyed 78 balloons in the London area on 14 September, tearing of fabric, winch failure, uprooting of pickets, and muddy sites, although these last three factors were becoming less common. Each barrage was controlled by a Barrage Commander, but emergency control was given to squadron COs, who could close-haul if weather conditions demanded. Unfortunately, the first aircraft brought down by the balloon barrages were British. On 20 November Oxford G-AFFM, which British Airways was operating for the Secretary of State for Air, fell foul of the Portsmouth barrage at Gosport and the pilot and first officer lost their lives. Another British aircraft hit the 931 Sqn. barrage near Portsmouth on 12 December and crashed, the crew of four being killed.

Their Majesties the King and Queen, ever anxious to see at first hand the effects of the war, visited a number of balloon sites in the London area on 19 October. At the first site they were received by AVM Boyd and by Air Cdre. J. G. Hearson of 30 Group, but before long the King was chatting to a corporal in charge of a balloon. The Queen, meanwhile, noticed a bicycle with food tins at the front and was told that it was part of a system for carrying hot meals to isolated sites in boxes insulated by hay. His Majesty commented on the number of First World War medals being worn and, asking what work had been carried on by the men

STANMORE PARK: THE WAR YEARS

before the war was told that all jobs from labourer to barrister were represented.

The first WAAF officer, Coy. Cdr. M. D. Henderson, was posted in on 26 October for administrative duties. It was, however, to be some time before the girls of the WAAF became accepted as balloon operators, as will be seen.

906 Sqn.'s headquarters left Stanmore on 18 December 1939 to move to 8 Hampstead Hill Gardens, London NW3, although, like 907 Sqn., it remained under the control of 3 Balloon Centre. Guarding Stanmore Park at various times during the latter part of 1939 were soldiers of the 2nd./18th Bn. Middlesex Regt., a detachment of the 2nd. Bn. London Irish Rifles and men of the 138th Field Regt. RA.

During 1939, RAF Stanmore Park became the home of a unit about which little has been revealed — the Operational Systems Research Section. Devoted to communications and technical problems on behalf of Fighter Command, the OSRS was commanded by Mr. (later Sir) Robert Watson Watt, the scientist who had been instrumental in developing radar, then referred to as Radio Direction Finding. Subsequently renamed Radar Research Section and finally Operational Research Section, the unit dealt with many significant projects, including operational systems of dealing with plotted information; night operations, including the co-ordination of radar and searchlights and the use of airborne radar; the development of ground radar equipment and the training of operators; and 'Identification Friend Or Foe' (IFF), which after the war was developed into the Secondary Surveillance Radar (SSR) which is the mainstay of modern air traffic control.

On the first day of 1940 Balloon Command had more balloons deployed and ready to fly, 895 in number, than at any previous time. However, on 13 January the Command's resources seemed about to be stretched, as the SASO and a Wg. Cdr. travelled to France to decide whether to deploy balloons at Le Havre and Boulogne

Cpl. Cyril Hooper of 3 Balloon Centre with his vehicle, used for transporting gas cylinders for barrage balloons. [Mrs. Eileen Hewitt]

as part of the Expeditionary Force. The decision was affirmative, and two weeks later, after the AOC, Air Cdre. W. J. Guilfoyle OBE MC, had spoken to the officers, 1 Barrage Balloon Wing was ordered to move. An advance party left early in February, and 912 Sqn. made the crossing from Dover to Dunkirk on 13 February. The Wing HQ and 924 Sqn. crossed from Southampton to Le Havre on 19 February, and the Wing was transferred to BEF that day.

While these moves were taking place, HQ Balloon Command itself moved from Manor House to premises in Old Church Lane, Stanmore, on 28 February. A further Group, 34 Group, was formed at Newcastle on 7 April 1940 to take over 18 and 19 Balloon Centres in Scotland.

March 1940 was a month in which several official visitors came to Stanmore Park, among them thirty members of the press from neutral countries who wished to meet the WAAF detachment. A number of high-ranking officers of the French Air

RAF BENTLEY PRIORY AND STANMORE PARK

Force also appeared, and AVM Boyd himself brought the Hungarian military attaché and his assistant on 20 March.

Defence!
Station defences were taken over on 20 April 1940 by RAF men, who replaced the 147th Regt. of Royal Horse Artillery. This move was the beginning of a trend which in January 1942 culminated in the formation of the RAF Regiment. To assist the somewhat inexperienced RAF men, officers of the Middlesex Regt. based at Mill Hill visited them on 18 May to discuss plans to counteract a possible parachute attack. Another helping hand was provided by the commander of the Local Defence Volunteers (which became the Home Guard), Maj. Wise, on 20 June.

Before general withdrawal of British forces from France began, 912 Sqn.'s eighteen officers and 340 other ranks returned to base on 24 May 1940. After reinforcement, the squadron left again, bound for Paris with 24 balloons on 11 June, but due to the worsening situation was recalled five days later.

Training of raw recruits as balloon operators began at Stanmore in April 1940, and by June they were being documented and kitted out and were undergoing basic training ('square-bashing') before learning how to man a balloon efficiently.

Visiting Balloon Command HQ on 15 July 1940 was Gp. Capt. HRH the Duke of Kent KG KT GCMG GCVO, who with the AOC-in-C inspected the Command's nerve centre and 3 Balloon Centre. At the end of that month 1466 balloons were deployed over the UK, including some from barges, trawlers and drifters off the coast of north-east England and Scotland.

With invasion from the air foremost in the minds of many people, the Station

Use of baloons was designed to protect structures on the ground by forcing the raiders to higher altitudes. In many cases it failed, with much damage resulting. The Houses of Parliament suffered from bomb-blast, with Marochetti's stature of Richard the Lionheart defying the enemy with a sword bent by the blast.

STANMORE PARK: THE WAR YEARS

The need to keep airborne enemy raiders as high or as far away from centres of population is clearly visible in this scene of destruction, somewhere in the East End of London.

Commander took to the air on 30 July 1940 to survey any possible landing grounds which had not already been obstructed. No records exist to say whether he found any, but a week later a tactical exercise was held with 300 men of the 2nd. Bn. Tower Hamlets Rifles simulating an enemy force dropped by parachute. Although the LDVs cooperated well with the RAF defenders, the Middlesex Regt. troops arrived too late!

Amid frequent air raids, all balloon training at Stanmore Park was halted temporarily on 18 September 1940. Recruits who had completed their basic training were posted to 906 and 907 Sqns., while 47 others carried on with 'square-bashing'. On 18 November, however, 75 recruits arrived for balloon training, although three nights earlier a stick of incendiary bombs had fallen through the roof of a winch and trailer shed, luckily without injury to personnel.

Maintenance of balloons was of interest to a number of US Army officers who visited 3 Balloon Centre on 28 October, among them Gen. Cheney, Maj. Gen. Yount, Maj. Edwards and Capt. Saville. Visits by members of the US Mission continued into 1941, when on 29 January the US Military Air Attaché, Capt. Vance, was at Stanmore Park. Yet another American visitor was Gen. Harmarr, who came on 22 May 1941 with the AOC-in-C, AM Sir Leslie Gossage. From an un-named South American country a party visited Stanmore on 7 August.

Air Training Corps established

Early in February 1941 a small headquarters staff for the newly-formed Air Training Corps — the organisation devoted then and now to the training of young people for possible careers in the RAF — took possession of *'Montrose'* in Gordon Avenue, Stanmore, the former home of ACM Dowding. An organisation founded in 1938 by the Air League of the British Empire and known as the Air Defence Cadet Corps had already established 200 squadrons, and 20,000 young boys had joined as cadets. By means of a Royal Warrant dated 1 February 1941 the Air Ministry took over the organisation with a view to considerable expansion. Commandant of the ATC was Air Cdre. J. A. Chamier, with Wg. Cdr. A. F. Ingram as his first assistant, although the latter was posted elsewhere in June and replaced by Wg. Cdr. G. H. Keat, who had been in charge of training. Rapid expansion of the Corps gave the small staff of officers, clerks and typists a great deal of work in such tasks as producing a training syllabus, rules and regulations, the issue of uniforms and other equipment and in financial matters. The working day was sixteen hours long, and soon a request was made that no telephone calls should be made to the HQ staff as they were just too busy! By the end of November 1941 nearly 6000 officers had been gazetted into the new organisation and vast quantities of uniform and technical equipment had been issued to the 1401 ATC squadrons which had been formed.

Growth of Balloon Command

By the end of 1940, Balloon Command had grown to encompass five Groups, 20 Balloon Centres, 66 squadrons, 2200 balloon sites and two mobile squadrons which were based at Cardington in Bedfordshire. At that time, all balloon operators were male, and it was not until WAAFs arrived at 939 Sqn. at Sheffield on 26 July 1941 that the situation changed.

They adapted quickly to the new life, some of them living in huts, some in floored tents.

The question of the most efficient distribution of barrage balloons was raised again on 13 February 1941, when Balloon Command was asked to re-examine the situation. It was suggested that barrages should be restricted to London, Liverpool, Birmingham and Bristol. The target was to launch 4000 balloons in four hours, not more than twice per month in London and once in the other areas. Total 'expenditure' would thus be limited to 20,000 balloons per month! Balloon Command was asked to develop an organisation on these lines in the near future. In retrospect, it is strange that a limit seems to have been placed on what was a viable means of protection from enemy raiders.

On 1 January 1942, the four Groups (31 Group having been merged into another Group) were flying 2334 balloons in total, including 173 on board ships.

By January 1943, the balloons at Stanmore were being used mainly for training purposes, especially by WAAFs involved in a substitution scheme

An amazing photograph that captured the mood and spirit of the times - and the reason why the country had to be defended...

They may have lost house and home, but for a few posssesions that could be salvaged , including an aspidistra in a pot and the clock from the mantleshelf...

STANMORE PARK: THE WAR YEARS

Three airmen (two corporals of mature years and an LAC) of 3 Balloon Centre at Stanmore Park, named on the original photograph as Jimmy, Ben and Stan. The building behind them is the MT section, which in 1997 still stands. The truck, RAF.35639, appears to be an American type made before the war by Reo or Dodge, while the other vehicle is a Chevrolet utility. [Mrs. Eileen Hewitt]

which was in course of being implemented so that airmen could be released to Bomber Command. Demands on the Command were decreasing, and in February 1943 the barrages at Londonderry, Belfast, Greenock and Blyth ceased to be operational, followed in March by Runcorn, Accrington and Barrow-in-Furness. In April the water-borne barrage in the mouth of the river Mersey was removed, all these reductions signifying the lessening effect of enemy air raids in northern areas. Along the south coast, however, barrages were being reinforced by August 1943. Stanmore's own balloons were by then not flown above an altitude of 300 feet or in visibility of less than one mile (1.6km.).

Taking part in the defence of Stanmore Park at this period of the war was 4143 AA Flight, RAF Regiment, but on 17 May 1943 the Flight was absorbed into 2718 Sqn., based at Hornchurch. Nevertheless, the Flight remained at Stanmore Park as a detachment.

Most of the summer of 1943 was spent by Balloon Command in implementing a reorganisation of balloon barrages and reductions in manpower from 50,000 to 30,000. In April it was decided that the future number of balloons would be 1638, which would be handled by 30,225 personnel — 1000 RAF officers, 200 WAAF officers, 17250 airmen and 11775 WAAFs, manning between them 1238 sites. This reorganisation, the sixth since war broke out, was completed on 1 August 1943.

In November 1943 Balloon Command was made aware of the requirements it would have to meet for Operation 'Overlord', the forthcoming invasion of France. Specifically, balloon units would be

RAF BENTLEY PRIORY AND STANMORE PARK

required on the invasion beaches. In the meantime, an even more pressing need was for a concentrated barrage to be set up on the North Downs, south of London. Titled Operation 'Crossbow', this barrage consisted of a curtain of 500 balloons placed at intervals of 66 yards (60m.) over a length of 20 miles (32km.). An impact probability of 1 in 10 was forecast. Two more Balloon Centres, at Biggin Hill and Gravesend, were formed in February 1944 to handle this project.

Stanmore Park home to the WAAF Central Band

Following a Minute sent by the Director of the WAAF to the Director-General of Personnel in October 1943, the Chief of the Air Staff gladly agreed to allow the formation of a WAAF Central Band. In March 1944 RAF Stanmore Park was chosen as the location of the new band, which was to be parented by 3 Balloon Centre. Wg. Cdr. R. P. O'Donnell of the Central Band of the RAF visited Stanmore from Uxbridge with a representative of the Director of the WAAF in April to begin forming the new band, and arrangements were made to post suitable airwomen to Stanmore Park. Bandmaster was Sgt. Sidney Ellison LRAM, a former member of the London Philharmonic Orchestra, who held auditions to select 53 airwomen who had played in bands at RAF Stations in many parts of the country. Good progress was made, the girls working at their own trades during the mornings and attending band practice each afternoon. They concentrated at first on drums, trumpets and cymbals and played for the parades which took place on 'Salute The Soldier' weeks and similar events, culminating in the eventual stand-down of Balloon Command.

Planning for 'Overlord' continued apace, combined with plans for 'Crossbow'.

Sgt. Sidney Ellison LRAM conducting the trumpeters of the WAAF Central Band during a rehearsal at their Stanmore Park base. [Mrs. E. Purle]

STANMORE PARK : THE WAR YEARS

The first outing for the WAAF Central Band, marching through Bushey on 3 June 1944 as part of 'Salute the Soldier' Week. [Mrs. E. Purle]

On 20 April 1944, 'P' Balloon Unit, formed to protect south coast ports during the invasion period, was deployed, while Beach Balloon Units completed battle-training courses at 6 Balloon Centre, Wythall before moving to 12 Balloon Centre at Titchfield, Hampshire, for further training and exercises. A prototype 40-foot (12.2m.) boat for the beach units had been approved several months beforehand.

A report dated 1 March 1944 provides information on the number of personnel administered by, but not necessarily based at, RAF Stanmore. The Headquarters unit of Balloon Command accounted for 240, 3 Balloon Centre for 653, 904/905 Sqn. 781, 906 Sqn. 829, 907/908 Sqn. 695, 954 Sqn. 252 and 956 Sqn. 243. In addition, for medical purposes the 703 staff of HQ 46 Group Transport Command, based at 'The Cedars', Uxbridge Road, Harrow Weald, were attached to Stanmore Park.

A virulent outbreak of smallpox at nearby Mount Vernon hospital, which was used by Stanmore-based personnel at times, caused the cessation of all leave and the beginning of a concentrated vaccination campaign on 4 March 1944. By the end of the following day, about 600 people had been 'jabbed', and the task continued until everyone had been dealt with.

'Buzz-bombs' versus balloons

With the arrival during the night of 15/16 June 1944 of the first V1 flying bombs, the North Downs barrage, the title of which had in the meantime been altered to Operation 'Curtain', was activated without delay. In five days 480 balloons were deployed, increased to 1000 and finally to 1750, stretching the resources to the limit. During July a large number of road convoys passed through Stanmore Park on their way to the anti-'Diver' (V1) balloon sites, causing a great strain on catering staff in particular. A great deal of help was provided by the men of 3 MT Coy., and equipment and balloon-repair personnel worked overtime to speed the convoys on their journeys. The task was not aided by the dropping of bombs fifty or so yards from a WAAF billet on the main site on 28 July, causing blast damage but no injuries. WAAFs working on balloon sites in the London area were now allowed to spend their leave days in the relative tranquility of Stanmore if they wished. Somewhat late in the day, personnel began digging slit trenches and erecting eight Anderson shelters in August, after a bomb had fallen on Hut 43.

For reasons which are not recorded, the twelve officers and 125 other ranks of 4770 Airfield Construction Flt. and 5513 and

RAF BENTLEY PRIORY AND STANMORE PARK

5523 Artisan Flts. (all part of 5025 Airfield Construction Sqn.) arrived at Stanmore Park on 22 August 1944. 4770 AC Flt. left on 9 September, when it was replaced by 4627 AC Flt. (part of 5027 AC Sqn.), while 5513 Flt. departed for Merston in Sussex and 5523 Flt. to Hendon on 21 September. Finally, 4627 AC Flt. left on 6 October.

Demise of the 'Blimps'

The anti-V1 campaign, however, was the final fling of balloon operations: in September the Air Ministry decided to close all barrages but to retain 800 balloons for possible deployment against any renewed attack by flying bombs. Within Balloon Command, 33 Group closed down on 26 October and 32 Group on 15 November, and disbandment or reallocation of squadrons took place. Another component of Balloon Command, known as 'M' Balloon Unit, which had distributed propaganda leaflets by balloon since the fall of France in 1940, was transferred to 2nd TAF on 7 November for operations on the Continent. The barrage protecting the river Scheldte in Holland was handed over to 85 Group, AEAF, on 11 December.

Within the framework of disbandment, Stanmore Park busied itself in November 1944 with disposal of large quantities of equipment. A Motor Transport Repair Unit (MTRU) was formed that month to overhaul for further use by other Commands all 800 motor-cycles and 15cwt. vans formerly used by Balloon Command, a former winch and trailer shed having been equipped as a workshop. This unit became known as 64 MTRU in December, and in January 1945 an additional task was set — the reconditioning of 2000 Ford V8 engines, at a rate of 20 per week.

Further down-grading of the balloon force came early in the new year with the closure of 30 Group on 7 January 1945.

A memorable occasion at RAF Stanmore Park — the official disbandment of Balloon Command on 5 February 1945. Leading the parade past Station Headquarters was the WAAF Central Band, and taking the salute was AM Sir Norman Bottomley KCB CIE DSO AFC. Above the parade a number of balloons flew, a reminder of the thousands which had formed the barrages over the United Kingdom during the war years. [via Mrs. B. Williams]

STANMORE PARK : THE WAR YEARS

Sir Archibald Sinclair inspecting the WAAF Central Band during the parade held at Stanmore Park on 5 February 1945 to mark the official disbandment of Balloon Command. The Drum Major, holding the mace, is wearing a four-stripe inverted chevron low on her arm to signify her position. [Mrs. E. Purle]

Two weeks later, the Air Ministry ordered the disposal of the remaining 800 balloons, but relented slightly, allowing 200 to be retained in four squadrons by the end of April, when Balloon Command was due to become a Wing of Fighter Command. With ultimate disbandment in sight, a stand-down parade was held at Stanmore on 5 February 1945, during which Lord Sherwood, the Under Secretary of State for Air, inspected a guard of honour and the Deputy Chief of the Air Staff, AM Sir Norman Bottomley KCB CIE DSO AFC, took the salute at a march-past. Other 'top brass' present that day were Sir Archibald Sinclair, the Air Minister, who said a few words to the assembled men and women, AVM W. C. Gill CB DSO MC TD DL (the AOC-in-C of Balloon Command), Air Comm. P. L. Lincoln CB DSO MC, his Deputy, and Gen. Sir Frederick Pile, the C-in-C of AA Command. The WAAF Central Band led the parade of three Flights of airmen, a contingent of Polish Air Force balloon personnel, twelve balloon carriers and trailers and twelve mobile winches. Afterwards, a Pathé Gazette newsreel of the event was shown in cinemas.

On 16 February twenty very smart WAAFs acted in a short newsreel film shot at Stanmore Park. All decided that they would not like to become film stars!

3 Balloon Centre was renamed Balloon Wing on 15 March 1945, and took over responsibility for the remaining squadrons — 901/5, 906/10, 951, 970, 998 and 999, plus five MT Repair Units, of which 64 MTRU was still based at Stanmore Park. By the end of March, 620 vehicles had been received by 64 MTRU, and 231 dealt with and despatched. The fall of a V2 rocket nearby on 22 March must have something of a shock to all Stanmore personnel, who

Personnel of 64 MTRU posed in front of the MT section, probably on VE-Day, as a few of the ladies are wearing exotic dresses. This building still exists at the time of writing (summer 1997). [Mrs. E. Purle]

RAF BENTLEY PRIORY AND STANMORE PARK

VE-Day was celebrated at Stanmore Park with understandable hilarity. Here members of the MT section have rigged up a makeshift 'float' carrying a placard marked 'Back to Civvys' [sic]. For some service personnel this turned out to be a little optimistic!
[Mrs. E. Purle]

at the time were steadily growing in number, totalling almost 1100. To occupy some of their free time, ENSA provided four concerts per month and there was a Station dance every week.

Hostilities over
VE Day, 8 May 1945, was celebrated at Stanmore Park in the same enthusiastic way as everywhere else. As soon as the good news was announced, the WAAF Central Band girls were hastily roused and paraded through the main street of Stanmore, many wearing WAAF-issue pyjamas! Next morning, after a parade to Stanmore parish church for a service conducted by the Vicar, Rev. Carpenter, many of the airmen and airwomen attended a concert given in the NAAFI by the Station orchestra during the afternoon and a Victory Dance in the evening. On VE Day + 1, a 'comic' procession wended its way around the Station before reaching the town, no doubt to the amazement of the residents! In the evening a fancy dress ball was held in the NAAFI, bringing to an end this joyful interlude.

During the spring of 1945 the WAAF Central Band spent a great deal of time

Another 'float' in the VE Day parade was provided by the WAAF Admin Section, who mad up this very strange bridal tableau!
[Mrs. E. Purle]

STANMORE PARK: THE WAR YEARS

In Brussels in July 1945 the girls of the WAAF Central Band were almost mobbed by thousands of cheering Belgians when the band performed on the occasion of RAF withdrawal from the country. Twenty-four squadrons of RAF fighters flew overhead during the parade. [Mrs. E. Purle]

and energy in playing at other RAF Stations and at football matches in the area. By this time there were eighteen drummers, 34 trumpeters and a Drum Major in the Band, which was coached by Flt. Sgt. E. Vollett. The Band's most exciting task, however, was a continental tour which began on 21 June, when the bandswomen flew in a Dakota aircraft from Hendon to Copenhagen to take part in the first post-war Danish Derby. Led by drum-major Mary Marsh, the girls marched just before the first race, enthralling the large crowd, and also showed their skills in a six-mile (9.6km.) route march which started at the former Gestapo headquarters. A few days later they were in Rotterdam, playing at a major football match and at an RAF air display, after which they returned to Denmark for

Another overseas trip made by the WAAF band was to Norway, a ground of bands-women coming ashore from their transport from Calshot - a 330 Squadron Sunderland, seen the the background. [Mrs. E. Purle]

RAF BENTLEY PRIORY AND STANMORE PARK

The Stanmore Park based WAAF Central Band stayed in Norway from 6 to 10 September 1945. They returned home to England aboard another Sunderland of 330 Squadron, this time WH:R, seen here arriving in the Oslo Fjord and moving up to an RAF pinnace. The mark in the centre of the picture was placed there by Eileem Purle and marks the location of the house of Vidkun Quisling, the Norwegian puppet Governor of behalf of the Nazis. [Mrs E.Purle]

another air display and an inspection by the Queen of Denmark. They then travelled to Belgium for the stand-down parade of 2nd TAF on 4 July, and another visit to Belgium, this time to attend the opening of an RAF Exhibition, followed on 20 July. In September the Band travelled to Oslo by flying-boat from RAF Calshot for the opening of the RAF Exhibition, during which the the girls were inspected by Crown Prince Olaf of Norway.

Balloon Command disbanded officially on 15 June 1945, and its officer structure was deleted. The MT Repair Units, including 64 MTRU at Stanmore, were transferred to the control of 43 Group pending disbandment. By July about 7500 wartime balloon sites had been returned to their owners without any major problems. In charge of this operation was Wg. Cdr. H. J. Ball, who had handled all the requisitioning and maintenance of sites since 1940, and Mr. H. M. Matthews, the Balloon Command Lands Agent. On 1 August 1945 all remaining balloon units were transferred to the control of Fighter Command, Balloon Wing itself following suit three weeks later.

RAF BENTLEY PRIORY AND STANMORE PARK

Chapter Seven
RAF Stanmore in Peacetime

In May 1945, when Balloon Command was in the throes of disbanding, the headquarters of 43 (Maintenance) Group arrived at Stanmore from Oxford. Its AOC at the time was AVM C. B. Cook CB CBE, who was replaced on 18 February 1946 by AVM T. Warne-Brown CBE DSC. Personnel in April 1946 totalled 537, of whom 39 were civilians. A part of the Stanmore Park site previously controlled by 232 Maintenance Unit was taken over in October 1946 by 3 MU, with headquarters at White City, which then became responsible for storing examples of equipment of our former enemies, including a number of interesting aircraft.

Also present, from the end of December 1945, was 1 RAF Film Production Unit, which arrived from its wartime base at Pinewood Studios, Iver Heath. Many films, some for training or morale-boosting purposes and others for historical records, had been produced by the unit over the years, and all would be of great interest today!

Many of the WAAFs of the Central (Volunteer) Band were now being demobilised, but on 15 October 1945, after a farewell dance at which Richard Murdoch and Kenneth Horne of the BBC's popular *'Much-Binding-in-the-Marsh'* programme entertained, the Band left Stanmore Park to move to Ternhill in Shropshire. The smart and enthusiastic performance of the girls was greatly missed in the Stanmore area!

New units formed

After a period of comparative inactivity, three new units came into being at Stanmore Park. First was 3604 Air Defence Unit of the RAuxAF, activated on 3 February 1947 as part of recently-reformed Reserve Command. By April, a steady flow of enquiries about service in the RAuxAF was being received, particularly from former WAAFs, but no instructions on the commencement of formal recruiting had been received. Commanding 3604 ADU was Wg. Cdr. J. Cherry CBE, who was appointed on 10 May.

Two pictures of an early post-war church parade of Stanmore Park personnel headed by the WAAF Central Band just before the girls were posted to RAF Ternhill. [Mrs. E. Purle]

RAF BENTLEY PRIORY AND STANMORE PARK

83 Reserve Centre was next to form, on 9 April 1947, with Wg. Cdr. P. G. Farr as Commandant. The Centre had been formed from 24 Reserve Centre at Woodley, near Reading, and at first it was accommodated in buildings once occupied by 3 Balloon Centre. Within ten days, however, the Centre moved into more permanent buildings.

Stanmore Park's third new unit, 2604 Light Anti-aircraft (LAA) Sqn., RAuxAF Regt., came into being on 12 May 1947, and like 3604 ADU was parented by 604 (County of Middlesex) Sqn., RAuxAF, which at that time was flying Spitfires from Hendon. Adjutant of the new squadron was Flt. Lt. A. Johnston. On the first day, Air Comm. E. D. Davies CBE and Wg. Cdr. R. C. Keary from 65 Group of Reserve Command visited and inspected a proposed 'town house', *Manor House* in Old Church Lane Stanmore, the headquarters of Balloon Command in the dark days of 1939. The unit was to share office space with 3604 ADU and would use a large hangar for vehicles and machine-guns. Two SNCO Bofors gun instructors, a corporal clerk and a fitter/armourer, all regular servicemen, were posted in on 1 June and a recruiting drive began.

43 Group's stay at Stanmore was fairly short, the unit completing a move to Hucknall, near Nottingham, by the end of June 1947. 212 Maintenance Unit, which had parented a sub-site at Stanmore, also withdrew at the end of June.

The question of a synthetic operations room for use by the trainee plotters of 3604 ADU was raised in June 1947, and it was decided that this facility would be built in a hangar. It was, however, sixteen months before work on this project began! A mobile GCI unit collected from 4 MU at Ruislip on 10 September consisted of six vehicles which were housed, for the time being, in 3604's hangar. Soon afterwards, interviews for personnel who wished to be commissioned were held, and eight RAF men and five WAAFs were selected.

Recruiting into 2604 Sqn. was very slow during the summer of 1947, and although several enquiries had been received nobody had been sworn in. To improve this situation, the RAF Regt. Demonstration Flight from Watchet came to Stanmore in September, and this ploy seems to have helped, as attestation began in October.

At 83 Reserve Centre, the year of 1948 began with 128 officers and 75 other ranks, all reservists, undergoing pilot training on Tiger Moth aircraft at 1 Reserve Flying School, Panshanger, near Welwyn Garden City. At Stanmore Park six buildings refurbished for evening use as lecture rooms came into use on 5 March, subjects covered being navigation, signals, engineering and armaments. A recruiting campaign for trainee navigators and signallers was held in April, and two twin-engined Anson aircraft were sent to Panshanger to enable these people to fly.

3604 ADU, meanwhile, concentrated on recruiting all ranks during the last part of 1947, and on 16 January 1948 a unit dance held in the NAAFI by all three Stanmore Park units helped the new recruits to get to know each other and to meet the AOC of 65 Group, who was the guest of honour. During March and April, trainees were sent on courses at Bawdsey — the home of RDF — and Trimley Heath.

Sqn. Ldr. H. Guy-Lewin assumed command of 2604 Sqn. on 21 January 1948, and from April training in ground combat, 40mm Bofors gunnery, small arms and field subjects took place each Monday evening.

Following a cocktail party organised by 604 Sqn. at *'Manor House'* on 27 June 1948, the official opening of the premises as the town headquarters of 2604 Sqn. and 3604 ADU took place next day. Recruiting drives at Edgware and Wealdstone by 3604 ADU were held in June, so that in September the unit, renamed 3604 Fighter Control Unit (FCU) that month, could go to the fighter airfield at Coltishall in Norfolk for its summer camp. 2604 Sqn. went to Watchet in Somerset for its two-week camp, which was attended by all personnel. On return, the squadron took part in a drive-past from Hayes to Ealing of all Territorial Army and Auxiliary units in Middlesex, the salute being taken by the

RAF STANMORE PARK IN PEACETIME

Chief of the Air Staff, Lord Tedder. Average strength of the squadron was now seven officers and 35 other ranks.

Recruitment of ground-based tradesmen to 83 Reserve Centre began in October 1948, and was slow at first. A 'Recruiting Ball' held at Wembley Town Hall by all three Stanmore units and 604 Sqn. on 17 December was well supported by the TA and was regarded as being very successful. 83 Reserve Centre's personnel numbers had risen to 283 officers and 164 other ranks by 1 January 1949, all of them carrying out flying training at Panshanger. Also at Stanmore Park from the autumn of 1948 were a few Jamaican airmen, some of whom in the weeks before Christmas received large parcels from their families at home, containing all sorts of good things not seen before by some of the Britons. Included in the packages were bottles of Jamaican rum, which the Jamaicans happily shared among their new friends, helping them to have one of the best Christmases they could remember!

After three years spent at Stanmore Park, 1 Film Production Unit closed down in February 1949, and the unit was downgraded to become a library holding the films made over the years. One assumes that by then either a plentiful supply of training and publicity films was available or that commercial concerns were being used to produce new material.

In March 1949 Fighter Command was notified that personnel would be required to form a guard of honour at the Royal Tournament to be held on 20 June. Training for this event was carried out over an eight-week period at Stanmore Park, NCOs of the RAF Regt. drilling the selected three officers, one Warrant Officer, four SNCOs and 72 other ranks.

As 3604 FCU was still suffering from a shortage of personnel, the unit sent an officer and 36 WAAFs to take part in a recruiting drive at Edgware and Hendon on 1 May 1949, with Gp. Capt. A. S. Dore DSO to take the salute. A similar event was held in Tottenham on 5 June. At the end of September, twelve officers and 87 other ranks flew from Northolt and Hendon to Colerne, from where they travelled to Rudloe Manor, near Bath, to take part in Exercise 'Bulldog'

2604 Sqn., changing its allegiance, was retitled on 1 June 1949, becoming 2600 (City of London) Sqn., RAuxAF Regt., parented by 600 Sqn., which was based at Biggin Hill and still flying Spitfires. 2600

Men of 2600 (City of London) Sqn., RAuxAF Regt., parading at Stanmore before leaving for their Summer Camp at RAF Watchet in Somerset in 1950. The gentleman with the flying boots on the right looks somewhat out of place! [Cllr. John Knight]

RAF BENTLEY PRIORY AND STANMORE PARK

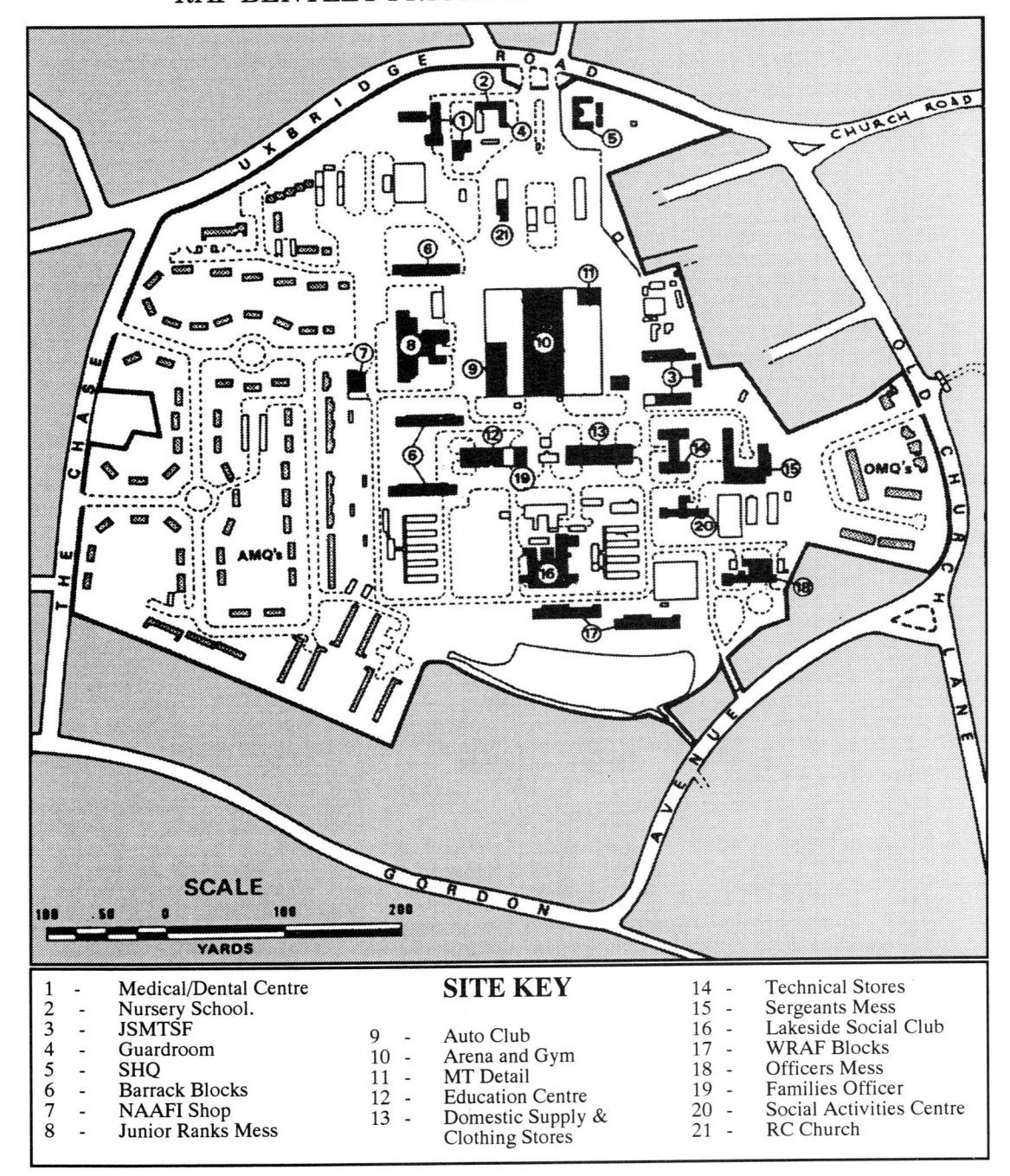

SITE KEY

1 - Medical/Dental Centre	9 - Auto Club	14 - Technical Stores
2 - Nursery School.	10 - Arena and Gym	15 - Sergeants Mess
3 - JSMTSF	11 - MT Detail	16 - Lakeside Social Club
4 - Guardroom	12 - Education Centre	17 - WRAF Blocks
5 - SHQ	13 - Domestic Supply & Clothing Stores	18 - Officers Mess
6 - Barrack Blocks		19 - Families Officer
7 - NAAFI Shop		20 - Social Activities Centre
8 - Junior Ranks Mess		21 - RC Church

Sqn. personnel attended summer camp at Watchet again that year, and on return learned that HM the Queen had consented to become Honorary Air Commodore to 600 and 2600 Sqns. from 3 August. A 'mobile training' weekend held at Abingdon on 29 October included a flight in a Hastings aircraft, which was much appreciated by all those taking part.

Moves were now in the air. On 19

RAF STANMORE PARK IN PEACETIME

October 1949, 3604 FCU's headquarters left Stanmore Park to set up in offices in Queen Square in London. 2600 Sqn. stayed put, however, and took part in the Lord Mayor's Procession in November. 3 MU, which was based at Milton in Berkshire, had occupied five hangars at Stanmore Park as a sub-site for storing captured Luftwaffe material, referred to as the German Air Force Equipment Centre, and on 1 November this was handed over to 4 MU, based at Ruislip. From there a detachment of airmen came to begin repairs to cased aircraft and engines, though details of these are tantalisingly omitted from official documents.

A new arrival at Stanmore Park on 1 December 1949 was the Fighter Command School of Ground Combat Training, previously the 11 Group SoGCT. There is reason to believe that this unit's stay was a short one, as it soon became a mobile unit, giving demonstrations at Fighter Command Stations. Replacing 3604 FCU, parts of Fighter Command HQ Unit — personnel of the orderly room, accounts, equipment and signals sections and some of the police — moved from Bentley Priory on 11 March 1950.

83 Reserve Centre carried on with its activities at both Stanmore Park and Panshanger, and by June 1950 conversion from the venerable Tiger Moth aircraft to new Chipmunks was almost complete. Flying personnel of 1 RFS at the end of January 1951 was 290 pilots (including five women); 102 navigators; 61 signallers; five flight engineers and thirteen gunners. At the Centre, 163 officers, 137 airmen and 43 airwomen looked after administration. There was such a shortage of sleeping accommodation that in February part of the Centre building was altered to provide extra space.

In December 1950 it was decided by Fighter Command that the most suitable site for the construction of a mock-up of a synthetic operations room was in balloon hangar 32 at Stanmore Park. A target date for completion of the mock-up was set for February 1951, but in fact work did not begin until the April. The old balloon hangars were the subject of criticism in February, when they were being repainted in a yellowish stone colour which was considered to make them an objectionable landmark and to be poor camouflage.

In May 1952 the highest number of hours ever flown by 1 RFS was attained, four of the flights being to Germany. Nevertheless, very soon the decision was taken at high level to close some of the Reserve Centres. After a dance in the Officers' Mess on 4 July, 83 RC disbanded on 28 July 1952, all its reservists being transferred to 4 RC at Rochester, Kent. 1 RFS at Panshanger, however, remained active until disbanding on 31 March 1953.

Based at Stanmore Park for a few months in 1953 was 681 Signals Unit, though the purpose of this unit's presence is unclear. In April 1954 three Reserve Flights, numbered 7172, 7194 and 7204, came into being at Stanmore Park to handle the growing number of reservists, particularly former National Servicemen who were usually obliged to carry out two weeks' training each year for a specified period of time.

To accommodate the personnel who took part in Operation 'Dividend' at Bentley Priory in July 1954, 453 beds were installed in the largest building at Stanmore Park, each bed standing on wooden blocks to prevent damage to a new floor. Individual folding canvas washbasins were set up in a hangar, while latrines were provided in tents. Stoves for heating water were also arranged in the open air. Although none of this could have been comfortable, it was only for ten days, and probably made a welcome break in the lives of many airmen, particularly reservists.

In February 1956 three specialised units, 3, 8 and 12 Joint Services Trials Units, arrived at Stanmore Park from RAF Ruislip, where they had been formed some months earlier. All three were destined to proceed to Edinburgh Field, Australia, to take part in missile trials at the Long Range Weapons Establishment at Woomera. In fact 8 JSTU left on 1 January 1957 and subsequently carried out trials of

RAF BENTLEY PRIORY AND STANMORE PARK

'Red Shoes', Thunderbird' and 'Red Duster' missiles, but 3 JSTU disbanded at Stanmore Park in April 1957. 12 JSTU departed for Australia on 10 July 1957 and worked on 'Blue Jay' and 'Firestreak' development there.

Further Reserve Flights were formed at Stanmore Park in 1956, 7142 Flt. in February and 7132 and 7133 Flts. in or by June. By February 1957, however, 7142 Flt. had disbanded, as had 7194 Flt. 7172 Ft. followed in October 1958. Other Reserve Flights lasted a little longer, 7133 Flt. until January 1964 and 7132 and 7204 Flts. until April of that year.

Stanmore Park's 'gate guardian' arrived on 20 May 1963 from Yatesbury, where it had served as an instructional airframe. A Gloster Javelin F(AW).1 night-fighter, XA553 is the oldest surviving Javelin of 435 built, and spent its flying career on development work at Gloster's Moreton Valence base. At the time of writing XA553 maintains its lonely vigil just inside the Station's gates, but its days in that capacity are clearly numbered.

Stanmore Park continued to serve as the Base Support Unit for 11 Group headquarters, Bentley Priory, and as the home of the Joint Services Mechanical Transport Servicing Flight (JSMTSF), which was responsible for carrying out major maintenance on vehicles of all three services based in the London area. For many years, however, Stanmore Park fulfilled the mundane function of providing domestic accommodation for service personnel based at Bentley Priory.

Freedom of the Borough

On 20 October 1988 RAF Stanmore Park was granted the Freedom of the London Borough of Harrow, but due to the prevailing security situation the Station's right to march through the Borough was postponed. Terrorists did indeed strike against the Station in 1990, when a rucksack containing an explosive device was thrown over the perimeter fence, but little damage was done and no injuries were caused.

Outline planning permission for the redevelopment of the site of RAF Stanmore Park for residential use with some open space was granted in January 1991, involving an area of 35.3 acres (14.3 ha.). It was noted at the time that there were two pairs of Grade II Listed gate piers at the Uxbridge Road and Gordon Avenue entrances, dating from the 19th century.

In April 1995 the Station finally took up the opportunity to march through the streets of the London Borough of Harrow in accordance with the Freedom granted seven years earlier. The Station always took pride in a close association with local organisations, and provided facilities for the Air Training Corps, the Scouts and Cubs, a youth club and a nursery school. An Indoor Sports Arena, constructed in the 1950s in a hangar formerly used to house balloon equipment, has for many years

Gate guardian at Stanmore Park for many years was this Javelin FAW.1, XA553 (7470M), which never saw RAF squadron service but was retained for trial purposes with its manufacturers, Gloster Aircraft. When photographed in May 1997 the aircraft's fate seemed uncertain. [author]

RAF STANMORE PARK IN PEACETIME

Members of the RAF Police under the command of Fg. Off. Vicky Craggs provided the guard of honour at Stanmore Park during the closure ceremony. [RAF Bentley Priory]

been used by service personnel stationed locally. Facilities were provided for a wide variety of sporting activities, with fixed seating for 400 and supplementary seats for another 800. In addition, Harrow 'Lions' used the facility regularly for 'It's a Knock-out' competitions for disabled people, and other organisations such as SSAFA held annual fairs there.

Final closure

Its usefulness greatly diminished in the aftermath of several reductions in manpower and increases in technology, RAF Stanmore Park officially closed on 1 April 1997. That day, AVM Cliff Spink and his ADC, Flt. Lt. Gary Headland, with the last Station Commander, Wg. Cdr. John Pearce and the Mayor of Harrow, Cllr. Alan Hamlin, took part in the closure ceremony, at which a guard of honour was provided by the RAF Police. The RAF ensign was presented to Wg. Cdr. Pearce by Sgt. Lynda Cook, and after nearly sixty years RAF Stanmore Park was no more. Officially, that is! In fact, domestic accommodation on the site will continue in use until new buildings at Bentley Priory become available from the end of 1998. Then Stanmore Park will be vacated, remaining buildings will be demolished and new houses will spring up. It is to be hoped that some of the new roads will be named after people who over the years contributed to the efforts of this important but little-known RAF Station and that residents of the new estate will realise the significance of the site.

RAF BENTLEY PRIORY AND STANMORE PARK

Wg. Cdr. John Pearce, the last Station Commander at RAF StanmorePark, walks in company with AVM Cliff Spink, Flt. Lt. Gary Headland and the Mayor of Harrow, Cllr. Alan Hamlin, led by the London Borough of Harrow's mace bearer, during the closure ceremony. [RAF Bentley Priory]

RAF BENTLEY PRIORY AND STANMORE PARK

Appendix One

Units

The lists below provide a guide to the units of the RAF which have been stationed at Bentley Priory and Stanmore Park over the years but should not be taken as comprehensive. There are question marks in the entries for some units, the result of vague or non-existent documentary evidence in those cases.

Bentley Priory

Unit	From	Date in	Date out	To
HQ Inland Area	Hillingdon Ho., Uxbridge	1.6.26	1.5.36	(became HQ Trg. Cmd.)
HQ Training Command	(ex HQ Inland Area)	1.5.36	10.7.36	Market Drayton
HQ Fighter Command	(formed)	14.7.36	15.11.43	(became ADGB)
Controllers' Trg. Unit	(formed)	10.6.40	15.6.40	Northolt
Controllers' Trg. Unit	Northolt	8.11.40	1945 ?	(disbanded)
2713 Sqn. RAF Regt.	(formed as 713 Sqn.)	19.12.41	9.43	High Wycombe
HQ AEAF	(formed)	15.11.43	15.10.44	(became SHAEF Rear)
ADGB	(ex HQ Fighter Cmd.)	15.11.43	16.10.44	(reverted to HQ Fighter Cmd.)
2718 Sqn. RAF Regt. det.	(ex 4143 AA Flt.)	17.5.43	4.44	?
2747 Sqn. RAF Regt.	?	4.44	?	?
AEAF Comms. Flt. det.	Heston	5.44	2.45	Heston
SHAEF (Rear)	(ex HQ AEAF)	16.10.44	2.45 ?	(disbanded)
HQ Fighter Command	(ex ADGB)	16.10.44	30.4.68	(disbanded)
2 Group Rear Element	(formed)	1.45	?	?
HQ Royal Observer Corps.	Uxbridge	2.51	1995	(disbanded)
Cent. School of Aircraft Recognition	(formed)	4.51	9.54	(disbanded)
Air Defence Ops. Centre	(formed)	2.53	1.3.71	High Wycombe
HQ 80 Wing	(formed)	1.8.53	15.3.57	(disbanded)
(*) Centralised Filter Plotting Centre	(formed)	2.54	8.56	(became Met. Raid Recog. Centre)
(*) Met. Raid Rec. Ctre.	(ex Cent. Filter Plot. Ctre)	8.56	4.57	(became Met. Air Defence Notification Centre)
(*) Met. Air Def. Not. Ctr.	(ex Met. Raid Rec. Ctre)	4.57	12.57	(became Air Def. Notification Centre [South])
(*) Air Def. Not. Ctre.(S)	(ex Met. Air Def. Not. Ctre)	12.57	9.58	(disbanded)
UK Air Traffic Services	?	6.59	1.1.61	(became HQ MATO)
HQ 165 Wing	?	9.59	10.59	?
HQ MATO	(ex UK ATS)	1.1.61	12.65	West Drayton ?
Control & Reporting Evaluation Team	(formed)	12.64	28.2.73	(disbanded)
HQ 11 Gp. Strike Cmd.	(formed)	30.4.68	1.4.96	(merged with HQ 18 Gp.)
Strike Cmd. HQ Admin.	(formed)	30.4.68	.73	High Wycombe
Systems Dev. Centre	(formed)	1.4.83	(current)	
SOCUK	(formed)	1.4.95	1.4.96	High Wycombe
HQ 11/18 Gp.	(merger of Groups)	1.4.96	(current)	
RAF Insp. of Flt. Safety	Adastral House	9.96	(current)	
Element of Air Warfare Centre		?	(current)	
Standby ADOC			(current)	

(*) signifies a unit working at Hll House, Stanmore Hill

135

RAF BENTLEY PRIORY AND STANMORE PARK

Stanmore Park

Unit	From	Date in	Date out	To
906 Sqn.	(formed)	12.38	18.12.39	London NW3
907 Sqn.	(formed)	12.38	1.9.39	Haringay
3 Balloon Centre	(formed)	1.39	15.3.45	(became Balloon Wing)
Balloon Command HQ	Kelvin Ho., London	1.9.39	15.6.45	(disbanded)
4770 Airfield Const. Flt.	?	22.8.44	9.9.44	?
5513 Artisan Flt.	?	22.8.44	21.9.44	Merston
5523 Artisan Flt.	?	22.8.44	21.9.44	Hendon
4627 Airfield Const. Flt.	?	9.9.44	6.10.44	?
MT Repair Unit	(formed)	11.44	12.44	(became 64 MTRU)
64 MT Repair Unit	(ex MTRU)	12.44	?	?
Balloon Wing	(ex 3 Balloon Centre)	15.3.45	20.8.45	(effectively disbanded)
HQ 43 Group	Oxford	1.5.45	29.6.47	Hucknall
232 MU sub-site	White City	4.46	10.46	(closed)
1 RAF Film Prod. Unit	Iver Heath	1.1.46	2.49	(became FPU Library)
3 MU sub-site	Milton	10.46	1.11.49	(became 4 MU sub-site)
BAFO UK Liaison Staff	(formed)	11.46	1.50	(disbanded)
3604 ADU	(formed)	3.2.47	6.48	(became 3604 FCU)
83 Reserve Centre	(formed)	9.4.47	28.7.52	(disbanded)
2604 Sqn., RAux AF Regt.	(formed)	12.5.47	1.6.49	(became 2600 Sqn.)
3604 FCU	(ex 3604 ADU)	6.48	19.10.49	Queen St., London
FPU Library	(ex 1 FPU)	2.49	8.57	(disbanded)
2600 Sqn., RAux AF Regt.	(ex 2604 Sqn.)	1.6.49	12.50	?
4 MU sub-site	(ex 3 MU sub-site)	1.11.49	3.57	(closed)
Ftr. Cmd. HQ Unit (part)	Bentley Priory	11.3.50	1.4.68	(Ftr. Cmd. disbanded)
265 Police Flt., RAFVR	?	12.50	2.52	?
681 Signals Unit	?	5.53	12.53	?
7172 Reserve Flt.	(formed)	4.54	10.58	(disbanded)
7194 Reserve Flt.	(formed)	4.54	2.57	(disbanded)
7204 Reserve Flt.	(formed)	4.54	4.64	(disbanded)
3 JSTU	Ruislip	1.2.56	1.1.57	Edinburgh Field, Aust.
8 JSTU	Ruislip	1.2.56	.57	Edinburgh Field, Aust.
12 JSTU	Ruislip	1.2.56	10.7.57	Edinburgh Field, Aust.
7142 Reserve Flt.	(formed)	2.56	2.57	(disbanded)
7132 Reserve Flt.	(formed)	6.56	4.64	(disbanded)
7133 Reserve Flt.	(formed)	6.56	1.64	(disbanded)
7131 Reserve Flt.	(formed)	6.63	?	(disbanded)

RAF BENTLEY PRIORY AND STANMORE PARK

Appendix Two
Air Officers Commanding

Date of appointment	Holder of office, with subsequent alterations to ranks

Fighter Command — Air Officers Commanding-in-Chief
14.7.36	AM Sir Hugh C. T. Dowding KCB GCVO CMG
	1.1.37: promoted to ACM
25.11.40	AM Sir W. Sholto Douglas KCB MC DFC
	1.7.42: promoted to ACM
28.11.42	AVM (acting AM) Trafford L. Leigh-Mallory KCB DSO
	1.12.42: promoted to AM
15.11.43	AVM (acting AM) Sir Roderick M. Hill KCB MC AFC
	16.8.44: promoted to AM
14.5.45	AVM (acting AM) Sir James M. Robb KBE GCB DSO DFC AFC
	1.1.46: promoted to AM
11.47	AM Sir William Elliott GCVO KCB KBE DFC
19.4.49	AVM (acting AM) Sir Basil E. Embry KBE GCB DSO DFC AFC
	1.1.51: promoted to AM
7.4.53	AVM (acting AM) Sir Dermot A. Boyle GCB KCVO KBE AFC
	1.1.54: promoted to AM
1.1.56	AVM (acting AM) Sir Hubert L Patch KCB CBE (temporary appointment)
8.8.56	AM Sir Thomas G. Pike GCB CBE DFC
	1.11.57: promoted to ACM
30.7.59	AVM (acting AM) Sir Hector D. McGregor KCB CBE DSO
	1.1.60: promoted to AM
8.5.62	AM Sir Douglas G. Morris KCB CBE DSO DFC
3.3.66 to 30.4.68	AVM (acting AM) Sir Frederick E. Rosier KCB CBE DSO
	1.7.66: promoted to AM

Balloon Command — Air Officers Commanding-in-Chief
7.11.38	AVM O. T. Boyd CB OBE MC AFC
	8.11.40: promoted to AM (acting)
1.12.40	AM E. L. Gossage KCB CVO DSO MC
1.2.44	Air Cdre. (acting AVM) W. C. C. Gell CB DSO MC TD
13.2.45 to 15.6.45	Air Cdre. P. L. Lincoln CB DSO MC

11 Group — Air Officers Commanding
30.4.68	AVM R. I Jones CB AFC
2.2.70	AVM Sir Ivor Broom KCB CBE DSO DFC AFC
6.12.72	ACM Sir Robert W. G. Freer CBE CBIM KCB
15.3.75	AVM W. Harbison CBE AFC CB
14.3.77	AVM D. P. Hall CBE AFC MRAeS
3.9.77	AVM P. A. Latham AFC
7.1.81	AVM P. R. Harding CB FBIM
11.8.82	AVM K. W. Hayr AFC CB
1.8.85	AVM M. J. D. Stear CBE MA
7.87	AVM R. H. Palin OBE MA
3.89	AVM Sir William Wratten KBE CB AFC
9.91	AVM J. S. Allison CBE
7.94 to 31.3.96	AVM A. J. C. Bagnall CB OBE

11/18 Group — Air Officers Commanding
1.4.96	AVM C. R. Spink CBE

RAF BENTLEY PRIORY AND STANMORE PARK

Appendix Three

Station Commanders

RAF Stanmore Park

Gp. Capt. E. A. Bald MC	13.9.39
Gp. Capt. R. F. S. Morton	16.8.41
Gp. Capt. E. L. Gower AFC	10.3.42
Gp. Capt. C. E. Benson CBE DSO	22.5.42
Gp. Capt. F. V. Drake MC	10.5.43
Gp. Capt. E. J. Davis TD	8.7.44
Gp. Capt. F. V. Drake MC	1.9.44
Wg. Cdr. R. L. Richmond OBE	1.12.44
Gp. Capt. R. B. Dowling	16.3.45 to 9.8.45
Wg. Cdr. E. Drudge MBE	14.12.45
Sqn. Ldr. S. A. Bennett	10.1.47
Sqn. Ldr. F. Barry-Taylor	9.1.48
Wg. Cdr. J. D. N. Beeston-Sidebottom AFC	6.12.48
Wg. Cdr. W. M. Collins DFC	20.8.51
Gp. Capt. R. A. C. Barclay OBE AFC	2.11.53
Wg. Cdr. D. W. Triptree AFC	1.9.54
Gp. Capt. J. M. Southwell DFC	27.5.57
Wg. Cdr. A. D. Forster DFC	29.6.59
Wg. Cdr. A. J. Payn OBE	5.2.62
Wg. Cdr. N. A. J. Mackie DSO DFC	8.6.64
Wg. Cdr. J. Rennie	13.10.67
Wg. Cdr. J. C. Douglas DFC	1.5.70
Wg. Cdr. R. W. Mathers DFC	10.1.73
Wg. Cdr. D. H. Wood AMBIM	2.6.75
Wg. Cdr. J. F. Jefferis MBE AMBIM	3.9.77
Wg. Cdr. P. C. Quinn	28.6.80
Wg. Cdr. M. J. Middlemist	9.12.81
Wg. Cdr. W. L. McKee	10.9.85
Wg. Cdr. D. M. Casey	8.4.88
Wg. Cdr. S. G. Appleton	11.4.90
Wg. Cdr. T. P. Buckley	3.7.92
Sqn. Ldr. P. C. Owen	13.2.95
Wg. Cdr. J. Pearce	3.4.95 to 1.4.97

RAF BENTLEY PRIORY AND STANMORE PARK

Appendix Four
Properties requisitioned for use by the RAF

The following list contains information on a number of the many properties in the Stanmore / Bentley Priory area taken over by the Air Ministry for use by the RAF. As far as the author is aware, no comprehensive list exists, and the one given has therefore been built up from scraps of information contained in other documents. The locations of some of the properties have proved elusive, as redevelopment has taken its toll of older buildings.

Name	Location	Used as	From	To
Children's Convalescent Home	Bushey Heath	17-bed sick quarters	1.9.39	
'Bushmead'	California Lane	ATS hostel	17.9.39	
'Rosary Priory'	Elstree Road	WAAF hostel	18.9.39	
'Otway Cottage'	do.	WAAF hostel	10.10.39	
'Two Oaks'	do.	WAAF hostel for 38	12.39	11.44
'County End'	Magpie Hall Road	Officers' quarters	3.9.39	12.44
Tanglewood School	Common Road	Billets for West Kent Regt.	3.9.39	14.10.39
		RAF hostel	14.10.39	
'Highfield'	Magpie Hall Road	22-bed WAAF sick quarters	9.42	
'Elderslea'	Magpie Hall Road	No.2 Officers' Mess	17.9.39	
1 and 3	Hartsbourne Road	ATS hostel	4.9.39	
'Arrochar'	do.	ATS hostel	10.39	
'The Warren'	Bushey High Road	WAAF hostel (opp. St. Peter's)	9.39	
78	do.	14-bed WAAF sick quarters	14.10.39	9.42
		??	9.42	4.45
'Honduras'	do.	WAAF sick quarters	10.11.39	
'Ad Astra'	Priory Drive	Offices for 247th AA Bn.	9.39	
'Barlogan'	do.	WAAF and ATS Officers' Mess	11.9.39	
'Woodham Ferrers'	do.	WAAF hostel for 30	12.39	
'High Trees'	London Rd., Stanmore	WAAF hostel for 30	11.12.39	
'Herondale'	Gordon Avenue	Used by 3 Balloon Centre	??	9.10.41
'Woodlands'	Clamp Hill	CTU	8.11.40	
'Gooden Gate' (42)	Stanmore Hill	AEAF: WAAF hostel	25.7.44	8.44
		Accomm. for Filter Room staff	8.44	
2 Halsbury Close	do.	Accomm. for Filter Room staff	8.44	
'East Haddon/Haven'	do.	AEAF: WAAF officers' quarters	25.7.44	
'Hill House'	do.	Metropolitan Sector Ops. Room		
'Kestrel Grove'	Hive Road	AEAF HQ Unit, then SHAEF Rear, then ROC	15.11.43	
'Holmebury'	do.	SHAEF Rear: used by officers after Stanmore Hall handed back to FC	2.45	??
'Glenthorn Lodge'	Common Road	CO's house	by 12.39	

139

RAF BENTLEY PRIORY AND STANMORE PARK

'The Cedars'	The Common	No.2 Officers' Mess?		
'Manor House'	Old Church Lane, Stanmore	HQ Balloon Command	1.9.39	28.2.40
		HQ Air Training Corps.	1940	1945
		HQ Fighter Command as residence for senior officers	1952	
'Yew Tree Cottage'	do.	HQ Balloon Cmd. (Officers' Mess)	2.9.39	
'Cherry Tree'	do.	do.	??	
'The Beeches'	do.	do.	??	
'Friars Mead'	do.	do.	??	
'The Dearne'	Uxbridge Rd., Stan.	CTU: billets for up to 80 airmen	10.42	
'Clodiagh'	do.	Operational Research Section, then No. 4 WAAF Officers' Mess		
'The Bowls'	do.	do.do.		
'Haydon Hill'	??	??	??	4.45
'Colne View'	??	??	??	??
'Pennimead'	Elstree	??	??	5.45
'The Oaks'	do.	??	??	5.45
'Homestead'	do.	??	??	5.45
'East Haddon'	do.	WAAF officers' quarters	8.44	
'The Thistles'	do.	??	??	8.44
'Duke Villa'	do.	??	??	8.44
'Down Villa'	do.	??	??	8.44
'Headmaster's House'	do.	??	??	8.44
'St. Mary Croft'	do.	??	??	8.44
'Whyteways'	Brookshill	??	??	??
Perry's Garage	High Road	??	??	??
'Goring'	??	??	??	??
'Hardwick'	??	??	??	??
'Kelso'	??	??	??	??
'Oaklands'	Uxbridge Road	??	??	??
14 Marsh Lane	Stanmore	??	??	??
16 Marsh Lane	do.	??	??	??
'The Rookery'	Stanmore Hill	AEAF HQ Unit: Officers' Mess for WAAF and WAAC	2.44	??
'Montrose'	Gordon Ave. Stanmore	Dowding's house	??	??
'Belmont'	??	Code & Cypher offices	?/	??
Little St. Margaret School	Merry Hill Rd., Bushey	AEAF: billets for 40	7.44 ?	??
Stanmore Hall	Wood Lane., Stanmore	AEAF Officers' Mess and accommodation for 90	??	2.45
'Elmdale'	Edgware	??	??	??
'White Lodge'	do.	??	??	??
15 and 17	Hillside Ave., Edgware	??	??	??

RAF BENTLEY PRIORY AND STANMORE PARK

Appendix Five
Abbreviations

The Royal Air Force, in common with the other Services, has long been a major user of abbreviations to denote ranks, units and decorations, and those applicable to this book, with abbreviations for a number of civilian decorations, are listed below. Where applicable, the meaning of an abbreviation has been supplemented by a further explanation.

AA	Anti-Aircraft
A&AEE	Aircraft & Armament Experimental Establishment [located at Martlesham Heath, Suffolk until the outbreak of war, then at Boscombe Down, Wiltshire]
AASF	Advanced Air Striking Force [an organisation heavily involved in the defence of France until June 1940]
AC	Airfield Construction
ACM	Air Chief Marshal [the second highest rank in the Royal Air Force]
AC1	Aircraftman 1st Class
AC2	Aircraftman 2nd Class [the lowest rank in the RAF]
ACW1	Aircraftwoman 1st Class
ACW2	Aircraftwoman 2nd Class [the lowest rank in the WAAF/WRAF]
ADC	Aide-de-Camp [a high-ranking officer's personal assistant]
ADGB	Air Defence of Great Britain [a body existing in the 1930s and in 1943]
ADNC (S)	Air Defence Notification Centre (South)
ADOC	Air Defence Operations Centre
ADU	Air Defence Unit
AEAF	Allied Expeditionary Air Force
AFC	Air Force Cross
AI	Airborne Interception [radar carried in intercepting aircraft]
Air Cdre.	Air Commodore
AM	Air Marshal [the rank below Air Chief Marshal]
AMWD	Air Ministry Works Directorate [commonly known as 'Works & Bricks']
AOC	Air Officer Commanding [usually in charge of a Group]
AOC-in-C	Air Officer Commanding in Chief [usually in charge of a Command, e.g. Fighter Command]
ARP	Air raid precautions [often referring to public or private shelters]
ASU	Aircraft Storage Unit
ATC	Air Traffic Control or Air Training Corps, depending on context.
ATCC	Air Traffic Control Centre
ATS	Auxiliary Territorial Service [female members of the Army]
ATSHQ	Air Traffic Services Headquarters
AuxAF	Auxiliary Air Force [postwar granted the Royal prefix]
AVM	Air Vice Marshal [the fourth highest rank in the Royal Air Force, below Air Marshal]
AW	Armstrong Whitworth [an aircraft manufacturer]
Batt.	Battery
BBC	British Broadcasting Corporation
BEF	British Expeditionary Force [in France in 1939/40]
BMEWS	Ballistic Missile Early Warning System
Bn.	Battalion
Brig. Gen.	Brigadier General [the USAAF rank equivalent to Air Cdre. in the RAF]
BSc	Bachelor of Science
Capt.	Captain [the British army or the USAAF rank equivalent to Flt. Lt. in the RAF or the Royal Navy equivalent of Gp. Capt. in the RAF]
CAS	Chief of the Air Staff [effectively the highest position open to a RAF officer]
CATOR	Combined Air Transport Operations Room
CB	Companion of the (Order of the) Bath
CBE	Commander of the (Order of the) British Empire
CH	Chain Home [coastal radar Stations]
CHL	Chain Home Low [coastal radar Stations scanning low altitudes]
CIE	Companion of (the Order of) the Indian Empire
C-in-C	Commander-in-Chief
Cllr.	Councillor [in local government]
CMG	Companion of (the Order of) St. Michael & St. George
CO	Commanding Officer
Col.	Colonel [the British army or USAAF equivalent of Gp. Capt. in the RAF]
Coy.	Company
Coy. Cdr.	Company Commander
C&R	Control & Reporting [the whole concept of interception of enemy aircraft by fighters]
CTU	Controllers' Training Unit
cwt.	hundredweight
DCAS	Deputy Chief of the Air Staff [see CAS]
DFC	Distinguished Flying Cross
DL	Deputy Lieutenant [of a County]
DRW	Defence Radio Warfare
DSC	Distinguished Service Cross
DSO	Distinguished Service Order
ENSA	Entertainments National Services Association [a body devoted to providing entertainment to the Forces throughout the world during the Second World War]
FANY	First Aid Nursing Yeomanry
FCU	Fighter Control Unit
Flg. Off.	Flying Officer [a rank; not necessarily an aircrew member]
Flt. Lt.	Flight Lieutenant
Flt. Off.	Flight Officer [a WAAF rank equivalent to Flt. Lt.]
Flt. Sgt.	Flight Sergeant [a senior NCO]
FTS	Flying Training School
GCB	(Knight) Grand Cross of the (Order of the) Bath

RAF BENTLEY PRIORY AND STANMORE PARK

GCI	Ground Controlled Interception	OBE	(Officer of the) Order of the British Empire
GCMG	(Knight) Grand Cross of the (Order of) St. Michael and St. George	OC	Observer Corps
		OSRS	Operational Systems Research Section
GCVO	Grand Cross of the (Royal) Victorian Order	OTU	Operational Training Unit
GOC-in-C	General Officer Commanding-in-Chief [an Army position]	PBX	Private Branch Exchange [telephones]
		QRA	Quick Reaction Alert
Gp. Capt.	Group Captain [the rank of most Station Commanders]	(R)	Reserve [applied to a squadron]
		RA	Royal Artillery
GPO	General Post Office [forerunner of British Telecom]	RAAF	Royal Australian Air Force
		RAFVR	Royal Air Force Volunteer Reserve
ha.	hectares [1 ha. = 2.47 acres]	RAuxAF	Royal Auxiliary Air Force
HF	High Frequency [pertaining to radio, usually for long-distance transmissions]	RC	Reserve Centre
		RCAF	Royal Canadian Air Force
HQ	Headquarters	RDF	Range & Direction Finding [the original name for radar]
HQIA	Headquarters Inland Area		
HQMATO	Headquarters Military Air Traffic Organisation	Regt.	Regiment
HRH	His (or Her) Royal Highness	Retd.	Retired
IFF	Identification: Friend or Foe [an electronic device carried in aircraft]	RFS	Reserve Flying School
		RNZAF	Royal New Zealand Air Force
IFS	Inspectorate of Flight Safety	ROC	Royal Observer Corps
JSMTSF	Joint Services Motor Transport Servicing Flight	R/T	Radio-telephone [voice transmissions by two-way radio]
JSTU	Joint Services Trials Flight		
KCB	Knight Commander of the (Order of the) Bath	Rt. Hon.	Right Honourable
KG	Knight of the (Order of the) Garter	SASO	Senior Air Staff Officer
kg.	kilogram(s)	SCOC	Strike Command Operations Centre
km.	kilometre(s)	SOCUK	Sector Operations Centre United Kingdom
kph	kilometres per hour	SoGCT	School of Ground Combat Training
KT	Knight of the Thistle	SHAEF	Supreme Headquarters Allied Expeditionary Force
LAA	Light Anti-Aircraft	sq.ft.	square feet
LAC	Leading aircraftman	sq.m.	square metres
lb.	pound [weight]	Sqn.	Squadron
LDV	Local Defence Volunteers [forerunners of the Home Guard]	Sqn. Ldr.	Squadron Leader
		SNCO	Senior Non-Commissioned Officer [i.e. Sergeant, Flight Sergeant and Warrant Officer]
LRAM	Licentiate of the Royal Academy of Music		
Lt. Cdr.	Lieutenant Commander [the Royal Navy rank equivalent to Sqn. Ldr. in the RAF]	SSQ	Station Sick Quarters
		SSR	Secondary Surveillance Radar
Lt. Col.	Lieutenant Colonel [the Army rank equivalent to Wg. Cdr. in the RAF]	SCOC	Strike Command Operations Centre
		STOL	Short take-off & landing [a term applied to an aircraft with that facility]
m.	metre(s)		
MA	Master of Arts	SU	Signals Unit
MADNC	Metropolitan Air Defence Notification Centre	TAF	Tactical Air Force
Maj.	Major [the British army or USAAF equivalent of Sqn. Ldr. in the RAF]	TD	Territorial Decoration
		Trg.	Training
Maj. Gen.	Major General [the British army or USAAF equivalent of Air Vice-Marshal in the RAF]	UFO	Unidentified Flying Object [often referred to as a 'flying saucer']
MBIM	Member of the British Institute of Management	UKATS	United Kingdom Air Traffic Services
MC	Military Cross	USAAF	United States Army Air Force [1941 - 1947]
MHz	Megahertz [measurement of radio wave frequency]	USAF	United States Air Force [post-1947]
Mk.	Mark [a term applied to aircraft sub-types]	VHF	Very High Frequency [pertaining to radio for short-range voice transmissions]
MLS	Movement Liaison Section		
mm.	millimetres	VIP	Very Important Person
MP	Member of Parliament	WAAC	Women's Army Air Corps [the US equivalent of the WAAF]
MRRC	Metropolitan Raid Recognition Centre		
MT	Motor Transport	WAAF	Women's Auxiliary Air Force [became WRAF in 1948]
MTRU	Motor Transport Repair Unit		
MU	Maintenance Unit [a term embracing a unit of the RAF which might be tasked with maintenance of aircraft or other equipment or with storage, disposal or salvage of products used by the Service]	Wg. Cdr.	Wing Commander
		WRAF	Women's Royal Air Force
		WRNS	Women's Royal Naval Service
		W/T	Wireless Telegraphy [radio transmission in Morse code]
NAAFI	Navy, Army & Air Force Institute	YMCA	Young Men's Christian Association
NATO	North Atlantic Treaty Organisation	YWCA	Young Women's Christian Association
NCO	Non-commissioned officer		